Common Ground

Second Language Acquisition Theory Goes to the Classroom

Common Ground

Second Language Acquisition Theory Goes to the Classroom

By Florencia G. Henshaw and Maris D. Hawkins

 *an imprint of*
Hackett Publishing Company, Inc.
Indianapolis/Cambridge

A Focus book

Focus an imprint of
Hackett Publishing Company

Cartoons on p. 13 and 110 reprinted by permission of Malachi Ray Rempen.
Cartoon on p. 74 reprinted by permission of Atlantic Feature Syndicate.
Cartoon on p. 142 reprinted by permission of Jorge Cham.
Langwich School cartoon on p. 186 by Jon Marks, in *English Teaching professional*
(102), published by Pavilion Publishing and Media Ltd. www.etprofessional.com.
Reproduced with kind permission.

25 24 23 22   9 10 11 12

For further information, please address
    Hackett Publishing Company, Inc.
    P.O. Box 44937
    Indianapolis, Indiana 46244-0937

www.hackettpublishing.com

Cover and interior designs by E. L. Wilson
Composition by Aptara, Inc.

Library of Congress Control Number: 2021945126

ISBN-13: 978-1-64793-006-6 (pbk.)
ISBN-13: 978-1-64793-007-3 (PDF ebook)

Contents

Section II: Interpretive Communication

Section III: Presentational and Interpersonal Communication

Preface

Goal and Scope

A major challenge in language teacher education is finding materials that clearly articulate the common ground among theoretical concepts, research findings, and classroom practices. Far too often, language pedagogy textbooks provide descriptions of a wide array of teaching methods and approaches, which sometimes appear to be based on conflicting theoretical underpinnings, leaving educators uncertain about the best course of action. Although a handful of titles promise to bridge the gap between theory and practice, they fall short when it comes to providing sufficient examples that make a direct connection between second language acquisition (SLA) principles and the reality of language classrooms.

As a result, practitioners are prone to making pedagogical decisions based only on their own experiences as language learners, personal beliefs, or students' expectations and preferences, which is something experts in the field caution against doing (Sato & Loewen, 2019). Rather than trying to address every aspect of SLA and pedagogy, which would result in an overwhelming amount of information, our overarching goal is to help world language educators understand how they can develop materials or implement classroom strategies that are informed by core principles of SLA.

Therefore, this book does not intend to provide readers with a survey of current approaches, a summary of the latest research, or a comprehensive overview of everything a language educator should know. Our priority is to keep our message concise and focused on applying SLA principles to the classroom, which is only one aspect of language teaching. We do not deny the importance of other aspects of the profession. Indeed, language teacher education comprises several different components. One of them is understanding how to help learners develop communicative ability in the target language, and that's the focus of our book.

Even though our title contains the word "theory" (singular) as a general way to refer to theoretical concepts and principles, there are indeed various theories of SLA. It is not our intention to portray SLA as a monolithic field of study or a set of universally accepted principles. What we have selected to include in this book is what we believe are fundamental aspects that language educators should understand and keep in mind when making decisions about material selection, course components, assessment practices, etc.

Organization

In the first section, we establish the foundation of what will guide the rest of the book. The first chapter outlines important definitions and general observations about the process of acquiring a second language. These observations have a direct connection to language instruction, and they will help readers discern the effectiveness of certain practices discussed later in the book. The second chapter is equally fundamental as the basis for effective instruction: goals and assessments based on the American Council on the Teaching of Foreign Languages (ACTFL 2012a) Proficiency Guidelines. Having a clear and realistic understanding of what we want students to be able to do at various levels is imperative to determine whether the steps we're taking are moving us in the right direction.

The rest of the book is organized around the three modes of communication, since that is our main focus. Given the importance of input for language acquisition, we dedicated two chapters to interpretive communication. Output-based communication modes (presentational and interpersonal) are grouped within their own section.

Each chapter is divided into the following sections:

- **What Do I Need to Know?** This section is where we present and discuss must-know information and concepts that should guide pedagogical practices. This section is peppered with text-box excerpts called "In case you were wondering," where we address some questions that we anticipate readers may have.
- **What Does It Look Like in the Classroom?** This section is where examples help readers visualize how to apply the principles and ideas discussed in the first section.
- **Now That You Know.** This section includes reflection, expansion, and application questions that could be used in a course, a reading group, or just to ignite a conversation via social media.

As much as we kept in mind the reality of the classroom throughout the book, in the Epilogue (aptly titled "Reality Check"), we delve further into some common concerns language educators have when trying to put principles into action, particularly when working under constraints that are out of their control.

To help our readers explore and expand on various topics directly or tangentially related to what we discuss in each chapter, we compiled web-based resources (e.g., webinars, videos, blog posts, podcasts, etc.) and suggestions for further reading on our companion site, which will be updated periodically. We also have a special section on strategies and suggestions for developing your Professional Learning Network.

Audience

This book was authored with language educators in mind, first and foremost. We have kept in mind their concerns and their questions, which we address throughout each chapter. Furthermore, we aimed to explain key concepts in a straightforward way, as if we were having a conversation with our readers. Even though it is not entirely jargon-free (i.e., some specific terms are good to know!), we have kept things as simple as possible, so as to not lose the forest for the trees. Throughout the book, we provide suggestions and examples for pre-service and in-service educators to adapt to their own contexts.

We believe this book will be particularly useful for:

- those who are beginning their journey toward understanding fundamental aspects of SLA.
- those who are looking to transition from traditional language teaching approaches to proficiency-based instruction.
- those who are grappling with how to make pedagogical decisions based on SLA principles.

Our intention is to offer various points of reflection for all language educators. We hope that our readers will be inspired by new ideas, reassured by familiar concepts, and challenged by thought-provoking questions.

Some Notes on Terminology

Second language acquisition (SLA): Even though this is the widely accepted name for the field, we are not implying that the target language is strictly the second language for all learners. We cannot and should not assume that learners are monolingual when entering our classroom. Whenever we mention "SLA," we actually mean "ALA" (additional language acquisition).

Target language: This is the term we will use to refer to the language you teach, as opposed to "second language" (L2), since some learners may have a different second language. Once again, the term "L2" assumes monolingualism on the part of the students.

Shared language: This is the term we will use to refer to the language that the teacher and students have in common, as opposed to "first language" or "L1," since it may not actually be the learners' or the teacher's first language. So, for example, in a Spanish 101 classroom in the United States, the shared language would likely be English; the teacher's L1 might be Spanish, and some of the students' L1 might be Korean, Polish, Hindi, etc. In some classrooms, there could be multiple shared languages, and in other classrooms, the target language is the only shared language. Our assumption for most of the examples is that there is at least one shared language, in addition to the target language.

Section I

SLA and Pedagogy

Chapter 1
Guiding Principles

Pre-test

Before reading this chapter, indicate whether the following statements are true or false, based on what you know or believe . . . for now!

- Acquisition is about developing the ability to communicate in the target language.
- Learners cannot control what they acquire, but teachers can.
- What happens in language classrooms is primarily "communicative practice," as opposed to true communication.
- Acquiring your first language is vastly different from acquiring a second language.
- Our role as language teachers is to explain how the language works.

Once you have finished, or while you are reading this chapter, verify your answers.

WHAT DO I NEED TO KNOW?

Defining Acquisition

A lot of pedagogy books talk about how to facilitate acquisition, but are we all on the same page with respect to what acquisition is? Without a clear understanding of what we are trying to achieve, it is quite difficult to know if we are going about it the best way. If someone asked you to define "language acquisition," would you feel confident and comfortable doing so? You're not alone if you're second-guessing yourself. It's like when someone asks you to define "culture" or "language."

The simplest definition of language acquisition is: the (mostly) implicit process of building a linguistic system by making form-meaning connections from the input. Basically, acquisition is what happens to you while you're busy understanding messages.

Why did we say "mostly" implicit? That's the best common ground we can find among a very complex discussion involving theoretical constructs that we won't get into (e.g., consciousness, awareness, etc.). We're trying to keep it simple here! What you should know is that it is a process we cannot consciously control. You can't wake up one day and say, "I'm going to acquire the present progressive today!" Neither teachers nor students have total control over what will and will not be acquired. Indeed, not everything from the input becomes part of the linguistic system, at least not in an immediate and predictable manner. As Lightbown and Spada (2008) said, "language acquisition is not an event that occurs in an instant or as a result of exposure to a language form, a language lesson, or corrective feedback" (p. 182). The reason why not everything becomes part of the system is that our brains cannot process it all at once. What gets and doesn't get processed? When we communicate, our main priority is meaning. Therefore, parts of the input that help us understand the message are *more likely* to get processed. And that is the two-sentence explanation of an incredibly complex phenomenon! In Chapter 3, we will discuss ways in which we can help learners get the most out of the input.

Notice also that the definition does not say anything about "learning to talk," "communicating," "mastering the language," etc., and that's because we should be careful about mixing "acquisition" with "skill development." If we approach language teaching as "let me explain how this works, then you practice it, and now you can use it," we are essentially expecting output without input. When we look at the roles of those two very important concepts in subsequent chapters, this distinction will become even clearer. For now, it is imperative to be on the same page about the following points:

- Input builds the system (acquisition).
- Output helps learners get better at accessing the system (skill development).
- No input? No output.

Output does not build the system, and neither does learning *about* the language. We don't acquire a language by learning its rules and applying them. We can express meaning accurately without being able to fully articulate any of the rules we just used. This is precisely why we said that acquisition is a (mostly) implicit process: The magic happens outside of your conscious zone.

That definition is the same for all languages. Now, we are not saying that all languages should be taught exactly the same way, with identical lesson plans simply translated from one language to the next. All we are saying is that no evidence suggests that only some languages can be acquired through input while others must be acquired by studying grammar rules. Naturalistic acquisition is possible for all languages, and that fact tells us that the roles of input, output, interaction, etc., are the same. And that's precisely what we're focusing on in this book. Even if one of the sample activities we suggest doesn't quite work for the language you teach, you can still apply the fundamental principles behind it.

In case you're wondering . . .

What about individual differences? Although it is undeniable that language development is not uniform across learners, the consensus about the impact of individual factors is not uniform either! First, it is difficult to measure internal and external factors, such as motivation, aptitude, and anxiety, in a reliable way; second, it is almost impossible to isolate some of these factors from others. More importantly, in the vast majority of educational settings, we teach a heterogeneous group of learners, and it is not realistic to expect individualized lesson plans. Nevertheless, it is beneficial to incorporate student choice whenever possible: free voluntary reading, assignment formats, prompts for final projects, etc. It is also important for instructors to understand their students' needs, preferences, and beliefs. This understanding doesn't mean changing your entire curriculum based on what the students want, but rather, taking time to address concerns, adding more variety in how you deliver the content, carving out some one-on-one time, and prioritizing learning over policies (e.g., accepting late work, letting students re-do assignments, etc.). We invite you to adapt, combine, and expand on the activity ideas we suggest in this book, so that your lessons have something to offer to every learner.

Defining Communication

We said that acquisition is the mostly implicit process of building a linguistic system, and we build this system through the interpretation of meaning, which is a key aspect of communication. Therefore, let's make sure we agree on what is and is not "communication," since that will guide the rest of the book.

Communication is probably the most famous of the 5 Cs within the World-Readiness Standards for Learning Languages (National Standards Collaborative Board, 2015). The other Cs are: cultures, comparisons, connections, and communities. The 5 Cs don't exist isolated from each other; they are very much interconnected. In fact, communication inevitably implies awareness of the audience, the purpose, the context, and all of its many pragmatic (and cultural!) intricacies. Although the focus of this book is mainly about helping learners develop a linguistic system that they can use to engage in communication, we do not deny the importance of the other Cs.

One of the best definitions of communication is VanPatten's (2017): "the expression, interpretation, and negotiation of meaning with a purpose in a given context" (p. 12). It is indeed a fantastic definition, but everyone seems to picture something different when it comes to the context and purpose. According to VanPatten (2017), the context of a language classroom cannot be altered: Students are students. Asking them to assume any other identity (tourists, restaurant customers, celebrities, etc.) would ignore the context, and therefore, the result would not be communication, rendering the purpose to be merely language practice. Instead, VanPatten emphasizes the need to respect the context of the classroom, where the purpose of communication is to learn about each other or the world around us. So, for instance, if you created an activity where one learner gives directions to another learner, who has to mark the route on a map and then indicate where they arrive, that wouldn't be true communication, according to VanPatten. And here's where things get tricky because proponents of Task-Based Language Teaching (TBLT) would say that is indeed a communicative task.

Is there common ground? Yes. First, we can all agree that communication should be what determines the linguistic resources we need, as opposed to the other way around. In other words, "communication . . . cannot be equated with first learning some vocabulary, then learning some grammar, and then finding something to talk about to use the grammar and vocabulary" (Lee & VanPatten, 2003, p. 1). Also, while it may be true that most of what happens in language classrooms could be considered "communicative practice," as opposed to true communication, nobody is saying that engaging in a task/activity where one learner provides directions to another has no value at all for language development. And, at the end of the day, our main goal is to help students communicate *outside* of the classroom, right?

So, at the risk of oversimplifying, we'll define communication as the purposeful interpretation and/or expression of meaning. For the context of the classroom, we propose these two questions to determine whether an activity involves communication:

- What information or content is being conveyed?
- What will the audience do with the information?

Let's look at some examples. Try to answer the two questions above for each of the following activities:

1) Learners read two short stories and decide which one they like best.
2) Learners write the list of ingredients of their favorite dish, and then the class has to guess which dish it is.
3) Learners underline all of the plural nouns in a paragraph.
4) Learners write down a series of sentences that the teacher reads to them (i.e., a dictation activity).
5) Learners form sentences based on clues like this: "Mary / walk / park / yesterday."

If you had a hard time answering both questions for the last three examples, that is because they do not involve communication. First, learners could do what you're asking them to do without understanding (i.e., without interpreting meaning). You could write down something you hear—to the best of your abilities—without knowing *what* you're writing. You could underline plural words without understanding what they mean. Sure, you can't do that without knowing anything at all about the language, but you can certainly get the activity done without focusing on meaning. For instance, if you asked students after one semester of Spanish to underline the plural nouns in the sentence *"¿Te gustan mis pantuflas?"* (Do you like my slippers?), they would underline *pantuflas* and they would be correct, even if they didn't know what the word means. And that is a problem because the linguistic system cannot be built without form-**meaning** connections. As for being purposeful, it's clear that the only reason why learners are doing the activities is to practice a particular form. Why else would learners need to form a sentence based on "Mary/walk/park/yesterday"? Nobody will do anything with that information.

On the other hand, the first two examples do involve the purposeful interpretation and/or expression of meaning:

- When learners read two short stories, they are interpreting meaning with the purpose of deciding which one they like best. It would be difficult to decide what story they like best if they had no clue about what they were reading.
- When learners write the list of ingredients of their favorite dish, they are expressing meaning with the purpose of conveying what goes into their favorite dish. And the rest of the class is interpreting meaning with the purpose of guessing what dish it is.

Throughout the book, you'll see that we will keep asking ourselves those two questions as we evaluate other common practices and activities in language classrooms.

The Three Modes of Communication

If you ask anyone to describe ways of communicating, they will likely mention the four skills: reading, writing, listening, and speaking. While that is a perfectly valid answer, a way to underscore the importance of context and purpose is to talk about the three modes of communication, which we summarize in the table below. Saying "interpretive written communication," for instance, makes it clearer that we are going beyond the cognitive process of decoding written symbols. However, this nomenclature does not mean that the four skills have disappeared; in fact, the ACTFL (2012a) Proficiency Guidelines are written for each of the four skills!

Mode	Role of students	Role of teacher	Examples
Interpretive	Understand, analyze, interpret meaningful content (written, aural, visual, or graphic).	Select and provide meaningful content, and scaffold comprehension and analysis.	Students read a story and draw pictures to illustrate it. Students listen to a series of suggestions for travelers, and then they decide if each one is a "do" or a "don't."
Presentational	Convey meaningful information for a given purpose to a particular audience.	Provide guidance and feedback on the "what" and "how" of the presentation (i.e., help learners "polish" their content).	Each student explains how to prepare their favorite dish; the audience later decides which of the recipes they are most and least likely to try. Each student writes a description of a house for rent on a discussion forum; their classmates write a reply guessing how much the rent is based on the information provided.
Interpersonal	Interact with an interlocutor to exchange meaningful information for a given purpose, either synchronously (in real time) or asynchronously (not in real time, delayed).	Create tasks or opportunities for students to exchange meaningful information or be a participant in the exchange.	Students work together to plan a party (e.g., they exchange opinions as to the date and time, whom to invite, etc.). Students post an image of something important to them (e.g., an object, place, person, etc.) on a discussion forum. Classmates write replies with questions and comments, and the student who posted the picture responds, poses new questions, and so on.

As you read the descriptions, you probably noticed a lot of overlap. For example, aren't we engaged in **interpreting** and **presenting** information while we engage in **interpersonal** communication? Absolutely! And isn't the audience engaging in **interpretive** communication while the presenter is engaged in **presentational** communication? Indeed they are, once again! In fact, a well-designed presentational task must consider the role of the audience.

In case you're wondering . . .

Is "interpretive communication" the same as "comprehension"? Indeed! ACTFL proposed the term "interpretive communication" to emphasize that comprehension shouldn't be just about literal retrieval of information from a text (e.g., right and wrong answers). Comprehension is much more than understanding words, and it inevitably involves interpretation: We understand messages based on our own knowledge, background, experiences, etc. In other words, when we comprehend something, it's our own interpretation of it! So, there is nothing wrong with saying "comprehension" when you refer to "interpretive communication," as long as you understand that comprehension goes well beyond the surface of what is explicitly stated.

As important as it is to understand what the three modes are, it's good to keep in mind what they are **not**:

- They are **not** tied to modality (oral versus written language). For example, you can have presentational writing and also presentational speaking. You can (and should!) have interpretive reading and interpretive listening. Even interpersonal communication can be either written or oral.
- They are **not** meant to happen in a linear way (e.g., you don't always have to do presentational before interpersonal). That being said, learners can't produce language without having had any input at all, and so it's always good to start your lessons with interpretive communication.
- They are **not** meant to correspond to different proficiency levels (e.g., interpersonal is for advanced; interpretive is for novice).
- They are **not** supposed to be approached as isolated components of a lesson. In fact, the more they build on each other, the better, as the following example shows:

Interpretive: Students read a series of classified ads of houses and apartments for rent, and then they answer some comprehension questions. Later, the instructor describes their own housing preferences, and students select one of the places described in the classified ads that they think would be the best option for their instructor.

Presentational: Students create a video tour describing one of the places for rent described in the classified ads, with additional information but without disclosing the location. Their classmates watch the videos and match each one with the corresponding ad.

Interpersonal: Students interview each other about their housing preferences (type, location, amenities, etc.). Then, they select the best and worst options for each other out of the places described in the video tours that their classmates created.

When it comes to the presentational and interpersonal modes, an important point to clarify is the issue of spontaneity versus preparation or "rehearsal." Presentational communication involves, by definition, some level of preparation. Even if you ask learners to do impromptu presentational writing activities (e.g., free writing), learners can craft their messages more carefully since writing is inherently more controlled than speaking. At the same time, prepared or rehearsed does not mean perfect or memorized. With respect to interpersonal communication, asynchronous exchanges in writing (e.g., several emails back and forth) are indeed interpersonal communication, and yet they are not spontaneous. Oral synchronous interaction can also involve some preparation or rehearsal ahead of time (e.g., a job interview), and that doesn't make it any less interpersonal. What interpersonal communication has at its core, whether written, oral, synchronous, or asynchronous, is an information gap between interlocutors: One person shouldn't know what the other one will say or ask. So, for example, if two learners are reciting a dialogue scripted ahead of time, it is not interpersonal communication. We will come back to this issue in Chapters 5 and 6 when we explore output and interaction.

First versus Second Language Acquisition

So far, we've been saying "language acquisition" without distinguishing whether we are talking about acquiring our first language (L1) or an additional language (L2+), and that's because many aspects of the process of building a linguistic system from input are the same for both L1 and L2+ acquisition. However, we should be very careful about assuming that whatever works for L1 acquisition can be readily applied to L2+ acquisition, let alone language teaching.

Here are some of the differences between L1 and L2+ acquisition:

- L2+ learners have a linguistic system already in place. This is probably the biggest difference that nobody disputes. A bilingual brain is not the same as a monolingual brain, and, as Grosjean (1989) said, a bilingual person is not two monolingual brains in one.
- Unlike monolingual L1 acquisition, L2+ learners make transfer errors, as well as other errors that are not from the influence of their L1 and are different from the type of developmental errors that we observe in L1 acquisition.
- Individual differences and external factors (e.g., motivation, aptitude, identity, etc.) may affect the outcome of L2+ acquisition; on the other hand, we can be fairly certain that babies acquire their L1 regardless of how motivated or extroverted they might be.
- The role of age: There seems to be a critical period for L1 acquisition but not necessarily for L2+ acquisition. This is certainly a heated debate among linguists, but based on what we know so far, acquiring an L2+ as an adult is more successful than acquiring your L1 as an adult (i.e., not having exposure to any languages until after age 12).

Some experts argue that any of these differences are irrelevant to the fact that the acquisition process is fundamentally the same. It is indeed important to note the following similarities between L1 and L2+ acquisition:

- Input is absolutely necessary; we develop a linguistic system making form-meaning connections, and without comprehensible input, that process cannot happen.
- Both L1 and L2+ learners exhibit U-shaped development, go through similar developmental stages, and make developmental errors (e.g., regularizing forms, like "foots" instead of "feet").
- In both cases, explicit instruction does not seem to alter the process. Teaching someone a rule doesn't mean they have acquired that feature, and that is equally true for L1 and L2+ acquisition.

So, what's the verdict? Although the two processes are not radically different, we can't quite conclude that L2+ acquisition is the *same* as L1 acquisition, especially when we consider that instructed L2+ acquisition (i.e., language classes) is vastly different from being surrounded by the language 24/7. There is a reason why we included the word "classroom" in the title of this book: As paramount as it is to understand the fundamentals of language acquisition, it is also important to acknowledge that language teaching doesn't take place in an ideal vacuum.

The Role and Challenges of Language Teachers

Language teaching is unlike any other type of teaching because language acquisition is not the same as learning anything else (e.g., dancing, playing an instrument, solving an equation, etc.). It is not about showing learners how to do it, and then helping them master it through repetitive practice. Repetition and imitation are not the driving forces of acquisition. Consider this evidence: We say lots of things—good or bad—that we've never heard or read before. True, some chunks are memorized based on frequent exposure and repetition (e.g., "how do you say . . . ?"), but when we communicate, we create with language. We don't simply repeat and recombine phrases we have memorized.

So, what is the role of the language teacher when it comes to facilitating language acquisition and development? To give students opportunities to engage in purposeful interpretation and expression of meaning. Essentially, the teacher needs to provide an answer to the two questions we listed above: What information or content is being conveyed, and what will others do with the information? Whether it is information you are giving to them, or they are providing to someone else, you should give them a clear reason for wanting to interpret or express meaning, and the reason cannot be about "practicing" language. Of course, language teachers have many other important roles.

In case you're wondering . . .

How do you know what to teach and when to teach it? One observation about second language acquisition that has been made since the 1980s is that there are developmental sequences: Learners appear to follow a predictable order in which they progress toward the acquisition of certain linguistic features, and this order is not random or influenced by explicit instruction. As tempting as it may be to think that you should organize your courses around developmental orders, this observation was never meant to be about what to teach when. Instead, "the value of developmental sequences research is in helping teachers adapt their expectations of how progress can be seen in something other than an increase in accuracy" (Lightbown, 2003, p. 6). You should organize your course around meaningful content and communication, as opposed to grammar structures. And always remember that just because you taught it, it doesn't mean they now know it!

Language textbooks have certainly conditioned us to believe that our course goals should revolve around language itself (e.g., regular and irregular verbs, different verb tenses, a list of words related to travel, etc.), and sometimes it's hard to imagine what classes could look like without a list of linguistic features to "cover." But when you think about it, most language courses start off with a communicative goal in mind, and the teacher helps the learners accomplish that goal: introducing yourself. Great! You probably would not start your very first day of classes with "today, we will learn present tense," right? It would be equally as awkward to start by saying: "Hello! Here's a list of words. Memorize them." So, why do we go from focusing on accomplishing a communicative task (e.g., introducing yourself) to explaining how the language works and giving them long word lists related to each topic? Why not keep our approach as communicative as it is on day 1?

Although it may seem straightforward to say that our role is to provide opportunities to engage meaningfully with the language, being a language educator has its own unique challenges. Perhaps the most challenging aspect is that when we create curricula and courses, we are inevitably rushing a very slow process. We want results, and we want them now. Textbooks don't help either: Their "thank-you-next" approach (i.e., every chapter covers something new) makes us think that after spending a couple of weeks on a specific aspect of language, our students now know it and are ready to move on to the next one. They don't. And they're not. This race to the finish line also makes educators want to find "shortcuts" (e.g., explaining simplified rules or coming up with mnemonic devices), thinking they are speeding up acquisition. Remember that acquisition is a mostly implicit process, so why would we approach it from an explicit standpoint (i.e., learning *about* the language)? The only real way to speed things up is to create more opportunities for communication (i.e., engaging meaningfully and purposefully with the language), both inside and outside of the classroom.

In a nutshell

Before we move on to classroom examples, summarize five main points from this chapter. What are your own takeaways?

_____

_____

_____

_____

_____

Would you like to learn more?
Go to **www.hackettpublishing.com/common-ground-resources**
for a list of suggested readings, webinars, and other resources.

What Does It Look Like in the Classroom?

Example 1: Transforming Grammar Drills

This example demonstrates how the teacher can modify a grammar drill, whose focus is to practice a particular structure (e.g., object pronouns, past tense), and turn it into a communicative activity, which involves the purposeful interpretation and expression of meaning. In the drill, the use of the targeted structure is forced and unnatural. By contrast, in the communicative activity, students can use any structures or words to communicate. In other words, the focus is no longer on practicing language, but rather on exchanging information with the purpose of determining something. We present two variations.

Proficiency level: Novice-high

Traditional Activity A: Drill Targeting Object Pronouns

Take turns asking each other the following questions. Answer in complete sentences, using the correct object pronoun, as needed. Follow the example.

> Example: *Do you wash dishes every day?*
> *Yes, I wash them every day.*

1) Do you sweep the floor every day?
2) Do you do the laundry every day?
3) Do you clean your room every day?
(more items like that)

Modified Activity

Step 1: Indicate on a scale from 1 to 5 how much you like or dislike doing the following chores:
1 = Please don't make me do it! → 5 = I don't mind at all and actually like it!

- Washing dishes
- Doing the laundry
- Cooking
- Taking out the trash
- Vacuuming
- Cleaning up

Step 2: Now, compare your answers with a classmate and summarize the information you learn here:

- Chores my classmate likes to do more than I do:
- Chores I like to do more than my classmate:
- Chores we both like:
- Chores we both dislike a lot:

Step 3: Based on that information, would you say you two would be good roommates?

Traditional Activity B: Drill Targeting Past Tense

Take turns asking each other the following questions. Answer in complete sentences. Follow the example.

Example: *Did you go to the store yesterday?*
                   Yes, I went to the store yesterday.

1) Did you talk to your friend yesterday?
2) Did you watch TV yesterday?
3) Did you exercise yesterday?
   (more items like that)

Modified Activity

Step 1: On this handout, check off the activities that you participated in last weekend:

Last weekend, I . . .

> . . . watched a TV show
> . . . studied for a test
> . . . read
> . . . went to a friend's house
> . . . went to the movie theater
> . . . ate out at a restaurant
> *(more items like that)*

Step 2: Now, compare your answers with a classmate and summarize the information you learn here:

- Activities my partner and I have in common:
- Activities neither of us participated in:
- Number of places I went:
- Number of places my partner went:

Step 3: Based on that information, who had a busier weekend? Who likes to go out and who prefers to stay at home?

Example 2: Transforming Dictation Activities

This example shows how the teacher can modify a dictation activity, where the focus is solely on listening and proper spelling, as opposed to meaning. The students don't need to understand what they are writing down; they just need to transcribe it accurately. The communicative activity still maintains the listening component for students to work on strengthening the aural-visual connection (i.e., matching how words sound and what they look like written down), but now the students need to understand what they are writing down to complete the rest of the activity.

Proficiency level: Novice-mid

Traditional Dictation

The teacher reads sentences, and the students write them down verbatim:

1) I love to run.
2) We like to play basketball.
3) They love to watch movies.
4) Do you like to play video games?

The teacher reads a few more sentences. At the end, the teacher shows students the sentences so they can correct any spelling errors on their piece of paper.

Modified Activity

Step 1: At the end of class, the teacher surveys students about their preferences out of a list of activities, which can be done on paper or using an online polling tool. Individually, students rank the activities from their favorite to least favorite.

- Play basketball
- Run
- Read

- Watch movies
- Play video games

The teacher collects all responses and tallies up the most popular to least popular activity in the class. However, the teacher does not reveal the results and tells students they will find out next class.

Step 2: The next day, the teacher does the dictation portion of the activity by reading the same list of activities and having students write it down.

- Play basketball
- Run
- Read
- Watch movies
- Play video games

Step 3: After looking at the list, students rank the activities based on what they think are the most popular and least popular activities, similar to the TV show *Family Feud*. The teacher asks students for a few predictions. Then, the teacher reveals the true answers. Finally, as an exit ticket, the students express whether or not they agree with the top choice.

Example 3: Interpretive Communication Activity

This example demonstrates how interpretive communication is scaffolded in class. The thematic unit revolves around dates and events. The teacher guides students primarily with questions that require little output on their part and facilitates comprehension using visuals (i.e., pictures, calendars, gestures). Although the teacher is doing most of the talking, which is expected at the novice level, the students are actively engaged with the content throughout the lesson. The teacher rarely says more than 30 words without asking the students to respond in some way.

Proficiency level: Novice-mid/high

> Teacher: Today we are going to talk about community events. What events do we have in our community?

The teacher shows options, next to pictures: football games, plays, festivals, concerts, etc.

> Students: Concerts!

> Teachers: Yes, we have a lot of concerts in our community. Do we have concerts every day of the week: Monday, Tuesday, Wednesday, Thursday, Friday, Saturday, and Sunday? Every day?

Students: No!

Teacher: Concerts are usually on what days? Fridays?

Students: Yes.

Teacher: Saturdays?

Students: Yes.

Teacher: Sundays?

Students: Yes . . . no . . .

Teacher: Not very common, right? Usually, concerts are on Fridays and Saturdays.

Let's look at this calendar of events in Sunnydale. (*Teacher displays a calendar of events for a community where the target language is spoken.*) Does Sunnydale have concerts, too?

Students: Yes! Saturday!

Teacher: That's right. There is a concert this Saturday (*points to the calendar*). How many of you like to go to concerts? Raise your hand.

Students raise their hands, and the teacher counts.

Teacher: About half of our class, fifty percent (*writes "50%" on the board*), like concerts. What type of music concerts do you like? Rock? Pop? Country?

Students: Pop!

Teacher. Me too! OK, but not everyone likes concerts. What other events are there for someone who likes music?

Students: Summer Festival on Sunday

Teacher: Ah, there's a festival! They probably have music, right? And what events do they have for someone who doesn't like music?

Students: Soccer game.

Teacher: That works! On the same day?

Students: Yes, Sunday.

Teacher: Who likes soccer? Raise your hand.

Students raise their hands, and the teacher counts.

Teacher: Who prefers football? Raise your hand.

Students raise their hands, and the teacher counts.

Teacher: Football is more popular in our class! Is football or soccer more popular in Sunnydale?

Students: Soccer.

Teacher: Yes, soccer. They have soccer games on Sundays. They have a lot of events on Sunday, right? In general, do they have more events on the weekend or during the week?

Students: The weekend.

Teacher: And that's very common. In our community, we have more events on the weekend, too. But we don't have identical events. Some things are different. Let's look at this calendar of events for our community.

The teacher provides students with copies of a calendar of events.

Teacher: Are there more sporting events in our community or in Sunnydale?

Students: Our community.

Teacher: That's true! OK, let's look at these other statements. Which community do they refer to? Read each one, and write down if it describes our community or Sunnydale.

The teacher displays statements like "There are more indoor than outdoor events," "There are more events on Fridays than Saturdays," "There are more sporting events," etc.

The lesson continues with other activities that engage learners in comprehension:

- Students use a Venn diagram to classify events that happen in both communities, as opposed to only one.
- Students suggest the best event for different people according to what they typically like and dislike, such as "someone who likes to be active."
- Students do a modified version of "two truths and a lie": Each student writes two events from the calendar that they want to attend and one they would not, by completing these sentences:
  Two events I want to attend: _____.
  One event I do not want to attend: _____.
  Each student reads the three events they chose, but not in order. The class has to guess which one they do not want to attend, based on what they know about their classmates. For example:
  Zach: soccer game, concert, and festival
  Teacher: Which one does he not want to attend?
  Rest of the class: concert!
  Teacher: Is that right, Zach?
  Zach: no, festival

Example 4: Presentational Communication Activity

This example serves to demonstrate how presentational communication is scaffolded in class. The teacher guides students through the process of writing a review of a local restaurant. Other alternatives include: reviews of a product, a TV show, a class, etc. This activity would take place after completing other interpretive communication activities with similar reviews.

Proficiency level: Novice-high/intermediate-low

> Teacher: Today we are going to talk about local restaurants. Restaurants in our town. What are some local restaurants?

Students name several local restaurants.

> Teacher: We have several! Do you like all of these restaurants?

> Some students: Yes!

> Other students: No!

> Teacher: We have different opinions, different preferences. Does it depend on the food?

> Some students: Yes!

> Teacher: It can also depend on the decor and the service. If the waiter is very slow and very mean . . . that's not good! Let's talk more about these three categories: food, decor, and service.

The teacher writes three columns with those headings on the board.

> Teacher: Now, choose one local restaurant. Only one! It can be your favorite, or it can be any restaurant you know. And it can be good, or it can be bad. Don't say the name of it. And don't write it down! Just think. Give me a "thumbs up" when you know which restaurant you want to write about.

Students think, give thumbs up.

> Teacher: Great! OK, first, let's talk about the food. It's the most important part, right? What words can you use to talk about food at a restaurant? Write a list.

The teacher gives students a minute to brainstorm on a piece of paper.

> Teacher: OK, what are some words to talk about food at a restaurant?

Students offer up words such as "delicious," "cold," "appetizer," "dessert," etc. The teacher writes the words on the board, under the "food" column.

Teacher: Very good! Now, write a few sentences or phrases describing the food in the restaurant you chose. Think about positive and negative aspects. If you love all the food there, then only positive. But if something is not very good, you need to say it.

Students write; the teacher walks around and helps students, if needed. The teacher can also add words to the list on the board if many students ask for the same or similar words. After students have finished with that part of the review, the same steps are repeated for "decor" and "service."

Teacher: OK, now take a few minutes to read everything you wrote. Read the sentences to yourself, slowly. Try to add a few more details. What other information can you give about the food, decor, and service of that restaurant? You can make changes, too, if you want.

Students re-read what they wrote and add information or make revisions; the teacher walks around and continues helping students.

Teacher: Now, exchange papers with a classmate. Read what your classmate wrote, and try to guess which restaurant they are talking about. Also, include the number of stars that make sense for that review. So, for example, if everything is great, that's probably five stars. But if anything was not very good, maybe it's four or even three.

Students read a classmate's review, guess the name of the restaurant, and assign a number of stars. Then, the original author confirms if they were right.

Example 5: Interpersonal Communication Activities

This example includes two variations of activities involving interpersonal communication, even when students do not have enough linguistic resources to hold a conversation on their own. Both examples could work with different age groups, although the second one might be a better fit for younger learners. The first activity is structured in a way that the teacher can help the students before they interact with each other. In the second activity, the teacher provides a model.

Proficiency level: Novice-high

Activity A: Daily Routine

Step 1: Complete these sentences in a way that describes your classmate's routine, based on what you think is probably true. Then, add on two more predictions about their routine.

My classmate . . .

> . . . wakes up at _____.
> . . . goes to school by _____.
> . . . eats lunch with _____.
> . . . goes to _____ after school.
> . . . eats _____ for dinner.
> . . . _____ before going to bed.
> . . . goes to bed at _____.
> (add another prediction here) _____.
> (add another prediction here) _____.

Step 2: Create questions for interviewing your classmate, and find out if what you wrote in Step 1 was right or not. For example, for the first item, you can ask, "Do you wake up at 7:00 a.m.?"

Step 3: Interview your classmate using the questions you wrote. Take notes of the answers if they don't match what you predicted in Step 1. If any of your predictions were not right, ask questions to get the information you need to correct the statement. For example:

> Student A: Do you wake up at seven?
> Student B: No.
> Student A: What time do you wake up?
> Student B: Six.

Step 4: Based on what items you got right and which ones you got wrong, do you know your classmate very well?

The teacher can also use the information they gathered to notice other trends or patterns among students' routines.

Activity B: Our Pets

Step 1: The teacher describes a pet without saying what type of animal it is, and students guess the animal. This activity would take place after students have had a chance to engage in interpretive activities related to pets, so the vocabulary won't be new. However, they can also have a list of common pets (i.e., the word in the target language next to the corresponding picture) to help them remember the words.

Teacher: I have a pet. Her name is Addy. She is big and very silly. She eats a lot of food! She is black and white, and she has a lot of hair. She likes to play and run on the beach. What type of animal do you think she is?

Student: Is she a cat?

Teacher: No, she is a BIG animal. And she runs on the beach . . .

Student: Is she a dog?

Teacher: Yes! Addy is a dog. Which of these pictures is Addy?

Teacher shows them three pictures of different dogs: one is brown, one is black and white, and another is all black.

Students: Number 3?

Teacher: Careful . . . Addy is black and white, remember?

Students: Number 2!

Teacher: Yes!

Step 2: Students work in pairs. One student asks questions to guess what pet(s) their classmate has. If a student does not have any pets, they could talk about a family member's pet or think about a pet they want to have. Depending on the level of the students, some additional scaffolding could be provided in the form of vocabulary, sentence starters, and sample questions, such as the following:

- What is your pet's name?
- Is your pet big, small, or medium?
- What color is your pet?
- What does your pet like to do? (Sleep, eat, play, run, go outside)

Then, students switch roles. As an option to extend the activity, the students could draw the animal based on their classmate's description.

Now That You Know

Discussion and Expansion Questions

1) It is not uncommon to hear some language educators justify their teaching approach based on these ideas:
    a) "This is how I learned, and I am very proficient."
    b) "Everyone learns differently, and for some students, drills are beneficial."

    What could be some potential issues with these justifications, based on the fundamental aspects of language acquisition we have outlined in this chapter?

2) Some scholars have suggested that learners acquire the language not as a result of instruction but *in spite of it*. How do you interpret that suggestion?

3) In this chapter, we discussed the role and challenges of language educators. What about language learners? What would you say is the role of a language learner in a communicative or proficiency-based classroom? And what are some of their challenges?

4) As a language teacher, you are bound to be asked what you think about language learning apps or sites (e.g., Duolingo, Rosetta Stone, etc.). Look into one of them, thinking about the fundamental aspects of language acquisition we delineated in this chapter. How much of a discrepancy is there between the way those apps/sites work and what you now know about language acquisition? Would you recommend any of them to a friend who wants to learn a language on their own, or would you suggest they do something else entirely?

5) Many language courses are organized around the "present-practice-produce (PPP)" approach. What is the underlying assumption of this approach, which contradicts one of the fundamental premises we outlined in this chapter? And why are each of the three Ps problematic based on what you now know about language acquisition?

6) The audio-lingual method (ALM) has been discredited by experts for several decades now, and yet some educators still incorporate some techniques that resemble ALM. Do some research online about the tenets and main features of ALM, and then explain how they contradict some fundamental aspects of language acquisition.

7) Imagine you encounter this post on social media. What would you respond knowing what you now know?

> *I have explained gender agreement so many times. We have done a lot of practice and played fun games matching nouns and adjectives. Most of my students do just fine when we play our games. However, my students are still forgetting to change the ending of the adjective when they speak or write. HELP! I don't know why they're still not getting it. To me, it's such a simple rule. What else can I do to help students remember to use it?*

8) Consider the following activity, which is popular in many language classes: *Create a menu for a new restaurant. Include at least five items for each of these categories: appetizers, entrées, desserts, and drinks.*
   In this chapter, we proposed two key questions to determine if an activity was indeed communicative. In this case, it is clear what information is being conveyed, but it is difficult to say what others will do with the information. What could be a way to transform that activity so that it has a concrete, clear purpose?

9) We said that the 5Cs are interconnected. Can you think of specific examples of connections between or among any of the 5Cs, relevant to the language you teach?

10) Indicate if the following examples constitute interpretive, presentational, or interpersonal communication. If you're struggling to classify one of them, explain why.

   a) Students create a survey for other students to respond to, and then they summarize the results.

   b) Students are tasked with planning a trip for the instructor, so they prepare some questions to find out more about the instructor's travel preferences and budget, and then interview them. Using that information, they plan the trip; the instructor later decides which option is best.

   c) The instructor explains their routine, step by step; the students have to act it out.

11) Here are the first two steps of a possible variation for one of the transformed grammar drills (see Example 1). What can you do as a third step so that the activity has a clear purpose? After completing Step 2, what could students do with that information? Don't copy the same Step 3 as the example presented earlier in the chapter!

Step 1: On the board, the teacher writes several columns: "I went to a friend's house," I played a sport," I studied," etc.

Step 2: Students come up to the board and write their names under the activities that apply to them.

Step 3: _____

12) In Example 2, we described one possibility for making a dictation activity meaningful. Here are other variations. Which one(s) would you incorporate into your classes? Would you modify anything?

Variation A: The teacher reads a series of true/false statements about a text students will be reading; students write them down verbatim, and they predict if the statements are true or false. Once the students have read the text, they confirm their answers.

Variation B: The teacher reads a series of sentences describing their daily routine; students write the sentences down verbatim and later put them in the correct chronological order, based on what they think is most logical. The teacher confirms if the order is right.

Variation C: The teacher reads a series of sentences describing different pieces of artwork, and students write them down verbatim. Later, the teacher displays the images and students match each description with the correct artwork.

Observation and Application Activities

1) Choose an interpersonal or presentational activity from a language textbook, and try to answer the two key questions we discussed in this chapter:

   a) What information or content is being conveyed?

   b) What will the audience do with the information?

   If needed, suggest a way to transform that activity so that you can provide a clear answer to both questions.

2) Observe two language classes at different levels (e.g., novice and intermediate, or intermediate and advanced), and take notes on the following:

   a) How were the three modes targeted in each class? Did you notice any differences between the two levels?

   b) What would you say the role of the instructor was in those two classes? Does the proficiency level of the students affect the instructor's role?

3) Choose one of the examples we explained in the section "What does it look like in the classroom?" and create your own for the language you teach and a topic that would be appropriate and interesting to your students. Alternatively, you can choose one of the examples and modify it to target a different proficiency level.

Chapter 2
Goals and Assessment

Pre-test

Before reading this chapter, indicate whether the following statements are true or false, based on what you know or believe . . . for now!

- Novice learners can use present tense; intermediate learners can use past tense.
- The ACTFL proficiency guidelines tell us how close students are to being native-like.
- The proficiency guidelines and Can-Do Statements are meant to help teachers plan their curriculum.
- Integrated Performance Assessments are a reliable way of determining someone's proficiency level.
- Proficiency is about how well learners can communicate, whereas performance is about how well they can apply the rules we have taught them.

Once you have finished, or while you are reading this chapter, verify your answers.

WHAT DO I NEED TO KNOW?

Understanding Proficiency Levels

Most times, when we think of "goals," we think of the product, the end result, the destination. But if we don't know our starting point, how do we know if we can really get there? If the distance between where we're starting and our destination is too large to be covered on half a tank of gas, then we need to make some adjustments. Understanding proficiency levels is crucial to knowing where we are, how realistic our goals are, and whether the steps we're taking are moving us in the right direction.

The framework we will use in this book to describe proficiency levels is known as the ACTFL (2012a) Proficiency Guidelines, which describe "what individuals can do with language in terms of speaking, writing, listening, and reading in real-world situations in a spontaneous and non-rehearsed context." ACTFL outlines four major levels: novice, intermediate, advanced, and superior. There is also "distinguished," but you don't need to worry about it . . . even certified testers are not "distinguished"! All 24 pages of the guidelines are publicly available, and we recommend reading them, but here, we will paraphrase and simplify what each level is about:

- **Novice:**
    - Can understand and produce words, lists, sentence fragments
    - Concrete, familiar topics
    - Mainly memorized material (chunks) or re-combined elements they read or heard; in other words, they can't quite create with language just yet
    - Almost always reactive: they respond, but struggle to ask questions
    - At times difficult to understand, even for language teachers

- **Intermediate:**
    - Can understand and produce sentences
    - Topics of direct personal relevance (inter-"me"-diate)
    - Mostly or all in present tense
    - Can handle simple communicative exchanges
    - Can ask questions
    - Comprehensible to language teachers

- **Advanced:**
    - Can understand and produce a paragraph (i.e., connected sentences in a logical or relatively coherent way)
    - Topics that go beyond personal and familiar
    - Can narrate and describe in past, present, future tenses
    - Increased accuracy and quantity of language
    - Comprehensible to just about anyone

- **Superior:**
    - Can understand and produce connected paragraphs
    - Broader range of topics, including abstract concepts and ideas
    - Can support opinions, hypothesize, consider various perspectives
    - Fabulous fluency and accuracy

In case you're wondering . . .

Is superior the same as "native speaker"? It is not. The ACTFL (2012a) Proficiency Guidelines were not written to compare "native" and "non-native" speakers. Monolingually raised native speakers are not necessarily rated as superior; in fact, many native speakers are rated as advanced-mid or advanced-high. That being said, we need to be conscious of the affective or emotional impact that proficiency scores may have on someone. For instance, if a heritage speaker of the language is told that their level is advanced-low, could that possibly contribute to exacerbating their linguistic insecurities? Food for thought!

Within the first three levels, there are also sublevels: low, mid, and high. And to put it as simply as possible, here's what each one means:

- "Low" implies that someone can sustain the level, but barely, and they never function at the next level.
- "Mid" implies that they can sustain the level fairly comfortably, and every now and then, they show some glimpses of the next level.
- "High" implies that they are so comfortable at that level that they're almost ready for the next one, and in fact, they exhibit characteristics of the next level most of the time, but they cannot sustain it.

To help you understand, let's take a look at how someone at each of the sublevels of intermediate would respond to the question "What's your routine like? Tell me about a typical day for you." Notice how both the quantity and quality of language increase with each sublevel:

- **Intermediate-low:** "I wake up six of the morning. I eat . . . um . . . the breakfast. I go work in office. I do a class, university class, at eight. After, I go the office again, and work. After, I go home. I go sleep at ten or eleven."
- **Intermediate-mid:** "I wake up at six every day. First, I drink coffee, much, much coffee! I eat a little breakfast: for example, apple or banana. Not much. At seven, I go to work. I work in the university. I teach one class at eight. I go back to my home at the . . . um . . . noon. Some days I go to gym, Tuesdays and Thursdays. At night, I watch TV and eat dinner. I like TV shows comedy. I usually go to sleep at ten or eleven."
- **Intermediate-high:** "During the . . . um . . . labor week, I wake up early, at six, but the weekends I like to sleep. First, I drink a big cup of coffee. I need a lot of coffee! I don't eat a lot for breakfast. I just . . . um . . . have, or, I grab . . . an apple or banana, and I eat it in the car,

while I go . . . going . . . while going to work. I leave the house more or less at seven. Very early! It takes twenty minutes to get to the university. I teach a class at eight. I go . . . I am back home between eleven thirty and noon, and I eat lunch. Some days I go to the gym after work, two times . . . a week. In the evenings, I watch the TV . . . while . . . eating . . . while I eat dinner. I go to bed usually about ten, sometimes more later. I like watching the TV at night. I like comedy shows."

A couple of important caveats: (1) the guidelines are written for each of the four skills, so it's not just about output; (2) you can't determine someone's proficiency level by how they answer one question. You need to look at the extent to which they can sustain the level across different topics.

In a typical classroom, you will have a mix of proficiency sublevels, and proficiency is not static, so you shouldn't worry about pinpointing the level of each student. Furthermore, someone's proficiency level tends to vary across communication modes: a student could be intermediate-mid when it comes to interpretive reading, but possibly only novice-high for interpersonal speaking. The main reason why we want you to understand in general terms what novice, intermediate, and advanced look like, coupled with the fundamental premises about acquisition from Chapter 1, is to help you establish clear and **realistic** goals for your lessons and curriculum. If you ask an intermediate-low learner to tell you a cohesive story about something memorable that happened during a trip (with good control of past tense), you are bound to be disappointed, and they are bound to feel frustrated and mistakenly conclude that they are just "not good at learning languages."

In case you're wondering . . .

What do I do if I have a group of students with very different proficiency levels from day 1? This is very common since adequate placement testing and practices are unfortunately quite rare. There are certainly some strategies that can be implemented if you have a mixed-level class, and we discuss some of them in the Epilogue. However, differentiated instruction is almost impossible if the proficiency differences among students are staggering: There is no feasible way of teaching novice and advanced learners at the same time. As a general rule, if learners are one major proficiency level away from each other (e.g., novice-high versus intermediate-high), then they should be in different courses. Teaching two completely different classes at once is not only unfair to teachers, but also a disservice to the students, and it should be addressed at the administrative level.

Moving up from one level to the next gets harder and takes longer as you get closer to the top. This means that if you are starting with "true beginners" (lower than novice-low!), it could be reasonable to get them to novice-high after a semester. But if your learners are intermediate-low, you probably won't be able to get them to intermediate-high in one semester. And if you have intermediate-high learners, you might need at least another year to reach advanced-mid, and many of them might not get there for a few more years. Of course, progressing from one level to the next doesn't happen just with time. It can only happen with multiple opportunities to engage in communication, as defined in Chapter 1.

Proficiency versus Performance

While the ACTFL (2012a) Proficiency Guidelines are great to know where we are (roughly) and where we'd like to go, the question is: How do we get there, and how do we make sure that we're heading in the right direction? That's where **performance** descriptors are helpful.

The basic distinction between proficiency and performance is that proficiency refers to what a person can do with the language in a spontaneous, real-world context, whereas performance is used to describe what a learner can do after having had the chance to "practice" similar communication activities or tasks in the context of the classroom. Indeed, performance is still about communication, and our expectations are still tied to the proficiency levels we described above. Performance is not about how accurately learners can fill in the blanks with verb conjugations.

When you compare the definitions of proficiency and performance, you might be tempted to think that proficiency is better because it seems more authentic and natural ("real-world," "unrehearsed"). However, the part about performance being "practiced" doesn't mean memorized or scripted. It simply means that learners have completed activities to help them acquire the language and develop the skills necessary to perform similar (not identical!) tasks.

So, for example, over the course of a unit on travel, students:

- identified key information in an infographic summarizing travel trends in a country where the target language is spoken.
- identified the main ideas in traveler reviews of tourist attractions and activities on a travel site, like Tripadvisor.
- listened to people express their travel preferences and selected the best option for them out of the offers listed on a travel-agency website.
- made inferences (i.e., deduced information) from a video showcasing various travel destinations in a country where the target language is spoken.

Can students, then, understand the main ideas and key information in travel brochures and promotional videos of other countries where the target language is spoken?

Educators don't have to choose between proficiency and performance. These two concepts go hand in hand. And the clearest way to see that is by reading the Can-Do Statements drafted by the National Council of State Supervisors for Languages (NCSSFL) and ACTFL. The Can-Do Statements basically tell you some of the **performance** indicators that correspond with each **proficiency** benchmark for the three modes. It is not an exhaustive list of activities for students to do at each level, and it is not meant to be a curriculum guide. It is a way for educators and learners to better grasp what we're aiming for at various proficiency levels.

Planning for Proficiency through Performance

Now that you understand what proficiency and performance refer to, let's look at the role they play in planning your curriculum, your course, your units, and your daily lessons. What we describe here is basically the world language adaptation of backward design, which Wiggins and McTighe (2005) outlined for general pedagogical purposes.

First, establish your proficiency target, keeping in mind where learners are starting and what level is reasonable and realistic to reach within the time frame you have in mind (i.e., one semester, a year, a two-year sequence, etc.). It's OK for your target to be a range, as long as it's not too broad.

Second, set goals for the course as a whole and for the thematic units within it. Think about what learners will be able to do with the language (i.e., the performance indicators in the Can-Do Statements) for each of the three modes. Your goals should focus on meaningful communication, and they should build on one another: recycle content and draw connections between units.

In case you're wondering . . .

How do you choose your thematic units? If you are not bound by a textbook or state-mandated curriculum and enjoy the freedom to choose any thematic units for your classes, then a couple of good places to start are: (1) network with other teachers and get advice about what topics have worked well for them with learners of a similar age range as yours; (2) survey your students! The only caveat about asking learners about their preferences is that sometimes they might not know how much they like a topic until they've had a chance to discuss it, so it is best not to limit your thematic units to student suggestions; instead, strive to expose them to new ideas. Another way of choosing your thematic units is based on texts (written, audiovisual, etc.). For example, a book or a movie can serve as the basis of your thematic unit, and from there, you can explore its historical context, sociocultural analysis, and connections to current events or the students' personal lives.

Third, determine how you will help your learners get there by planning your daily lessons around specific communicative goals that are measurable and make sense for both your unit goals and your course goals. And here's where having a clear grasp of the fundamentals of language acquisition is crucial. Although it might be tempting to think of what vocab and grammar structures you'll need to "cover" or "teach," remember that language acquisition is the mostly *implicit* process of building a linguistic system in your head by making *form-meaning* connections from the input. Therefore, the input you provide should be relevant to the topic and tasks at hand.

Equally important to setting goals is establishing how you will determine whether you have reached them or not. The evidence, as a whole, should help you figure out if learners can do something consistently (i.e., not just on the final exam), in different ways (i.e., not always true/false), and across a range of topics (i.e., your thematic units). Of course, each activity will also have its own goal, along with a measurable way for you to determine the extent to which learners successfully accomplished it. Let's take a look at some examples.

Proficiency level: Intermediate-low

Interpretive communication performance indicator: I can identify the main ideas and key information in authentic informational texts.

Thematic unit: Travel

Thematic unit goals: I can . . .	Evidence: How will you know they can do that?
. . . identify key information in an infographic summarizing travel trends in a country where the target language is spoken.	By establishing simple comparisons with trends in their own country (e.g., similar, different)
. . . identify main ideas in a short blog post about traveling.	By answering comprehension questions, and then selecting pictures that would illustrate them adequately
. . . identify the main ideas in traveler reviews of tourist attractions and activities on a travel site.	By assigning a number of stars based on the content of the review, and then deciding which tourist attraction or activity they would choose for their own trip
. . . identify the main ideas and key information in a promotional video for a hotel.	By making inferences about the guests and the price of a room, and justifying those inferences based on information in the video

Keep in mind the following as you establish your "evidence" for any of the three modes:

- **Is it measurable?** There should be no room for misinterpretation with respect to what the evidence looks like, and it should be clear whether the learners have or have not yet reached that goal. Use action verbs to depict concrete outcomes: describe, compare, list, write, etc.
- **Is it appropriate for the level?** Learners shouldn't be asked to do something that requires abilities they don't have yet or that go beyond the targeted level. For example, novice learners are not yet able to write a summary paragraph in the target language as a way to demonstrate understanding of a text.
- **Is it reliable?** What you're asking learners to do should be directly dependent on what they can do with the language in that particular mode. For instance, if they are not yet able to identify the main ideas in traveler reviews, then they won't be able to assign a number of stars to each one.

The examples of "evidence" we provided above can and should be done without any grades or scores attached to them. At the same time, we cannot deny the relationship between goals, assessments, and grades in just about all educational institutions: We tend to think of grades as a reflection of how well students were able to meet the instructional goals or reach the intended level. So, let's talk about the elephant in the room: tests and grades.

Assessing and Evaluating Performance

Although assessment is associated with something that happens *after* instruction, and thus, it tends to be the final chapter of pedagogy books, backwards design is all about starting with your end goal in mind, and it is absolutely crucial for assessment and instruction to inform each other. In other words, assessment is not something you figure out based on what you taught.

Another reason why it is important to talk about assessment early on is that testing and instruction should be closely aligned. The tasks students are asked to perform as part of any assessments should mirror what students have been doing in class, and at the same time, in-class activities should be informed by assessment results. We have seen the following scenario of misalignment between instruction and assessment far too often: Well-intended teachers who want to move away from traditional instruction incorporate "communicative" activities in class, but the tests remain all about correctly labeling items from a long vocab list, filling in the blanks with specific verb forms, etc. When students get low scores, teachers end up concluding something along the lines of "input doesn't work," "communicative activities are not enough," or "students need more grammar practice." As shocking as it will be to read the following statement, it is true: If you want students to do well on exams that test their memorization skills and correct application of rules, then mechanical practice might be the way to go. You won't find a section on "how to design good drills" or "fun ways to practice verb conjugation" in this book, though, and that's because we are assuming that your assessments and instructional decisions are guided by the overarching goal of determining the extent to which a learner can engage in communication (i.e., the purposeful interpretation and expression of meaning).

Some educators feel that evaluating students is in itself problematic, and most times, the concern stems from equating "tests" with decontextualized, discrete-point questions that only aim to gauge learners' knowledge of grammar rules and isolated vocab items, which is indeed problematic. However, eliminating all forms of evaluation seems unrealistic for the majority of instructional contexts. Plus, assessing what learners can do with the language can be valuable to determine to what extent program goals are being met, help learners have a better understanding of their abilities, and inform educators about their students' instructional needs.

Indeed, a key aspect of successful assessment practices, often implied but not always mentioned, is to have the flexibility to adjust instructional content and strategies based on how learners are performing on formative assessments, which are meant to inform both the instructor and the student with respect to language development and progress toward communicative goals: What can learners do minimally, what can they do comfortably and fully, and what are they not yet able to do? Simply assigning grades won't have much of an impact on their language development. Instead, the instructor should provide learners with the support they need based on their performance. This is why it is necessary to have multiple ways of assessing students, as opposed to putting all their eggs in the final exam basket.

Pros and Cons of Integrated Performance Assessments

One approach to assessment that embodies all of the key qualities we have discussed above is the ACTFL's Integrated Performance Assessment (IPA), which consists of three interconnected tasks aimed at determining the students' ability to engage in interpretive, interpersonal, and presentational communication. It bears pointing out that IPAs are not the only option when it comes to performance-based assessments, nor are they the only alternative to discrete-point tests. However, it is no secret that educators have embraced IPAs as a breath of fresh air, and indeed they are, so let's dive in and dissect the ins and outs of IPAs.

Each IPA has an overarching context that helps learners understand the "why" and "what" of the three tasks, and this context is known as the "task overview" (Adair-Hauck, et al., 2013). All tasks revolve around the same theme, which often stems from one or more essential questions (e.g., "What is the role of animals in our society?"). Unlike other assessment types, where each component typically can stand alone, the three tasks that comprise one IPA build on each other in a way that students need to accomplish one so they can do the next. Usually, students inform themselves through reading or listening/viewing (interpretive), exchange ideas on that topic with a partner (interpersonal), and present a product related to what they have learned or found out (presentational).

Other hallmarks of IPAs are:

- Authenticity permeates every aspect of an IPA. For the interpretive communication task, the text (oral or written) is authentic (i.e., not created or modified for learners). The interpersonal and presentational tasks reflect "real-world" situations and communicative functions; that is, learners accomplish something that teachers would reasonably expect their students to do in real life, and it should be something that resonates with them. For instance, high school students often organize fundraisers, so the interpersonal and presentational tasks could involve something to that effect.

- Feedback and support are provided throughout, as opposed to at the end of the entire assessment. For example, feedback on their performance on the interpretive portion (e.g., comprehension of a text) is necessary and helpful before learners engage in an interpersonal discussion on the content or ideas of the text. The type and format of the feedback given throughout an IPA is unique: It is co-constructed by both the instructor and the students through guiding questions, self-assessment, and reflection. The purpose of the feedback is to help learners understand their performance and improve (i.e., continue to develop their language skills), and not merely justify the grade they received. Furthermore, feedback is guided by a rubric that aligns with both the ACTFL (2012b) Performance Descriptors for Language Learners and the ACTFL (2012a) Proficiency Guidelines.

IPAs are not meant to be "add-ons" to a traditional curriculum. Successfully implementing IPAs requires significant changes, from selecting thematic units to properly preparing students for the types of tasks involved in IPAs. Furthermore, teachers should have access to the necessary training to have a firm grasp on performance at various proficiency levels, and they should be adequately supported to adapt their lessons to the needs of their students, based on assessment results. The information summarized here is only the tip of the iceberg.

In case you're wondering . . .

How much class time do you dedicate to one IPA? It is hard to give a specific answer without considering what level you teach and what tasks you have in mind. However, we can tell you some things for now. First and foremost, each phase is supposed to be followed by feedback that the students can use for the next part, so you can't quite do all three parts in one sitting. Teachers tend to space them out; for instance, you can do the interpretive portion earlier in the unit, the interpersonal part a few days later, and then the presentational task at the very end. In between, you would continue discussing the topic, making sure learners have no lingering confusion from the interpretive task and allowing them to develop their interpersonal and presentational communication skills. Something else to consider is that part of the presentational assessment could be completed at home (e.g., preparing slides for their oral presentation), while the interpretive and interpersonal portions typically would take place during class time. Of course, if you are concerned about potential academic dishonesty and want to be 100% sure their work is indeed their own, you could have students complete all parts of the IPA in class.

In addition to the challenges associated with the time-consuming nature of co-constructed feedback, a few other aspects of IPAs could give pause to some language educators:

- Finding multiple authentic, unmodified, and age-appropriate resources for novice learners to complete interpretive communication tasks (as preparation for the IPA and for the IPA itself) can be challenging, especially for less commonly taught languages. Moreover, from a language acquisition standpoint, comprehensibility should be more important than authenticity. We will discuss authentic resources at greater length in Chapter 3.
- In most sample IPAs, the interpersonal and presentational portions appear to be less developed or specific than the interpretive portion. On the one hand, interpretive communication skills are assessed through a myriad of questions strategically designed to

inquire about keyword recognition, main idea, supporting details, organizational features, inferences, cultural comparisons, and personal reaction to the text. On the other hand, the interpersonal and presentational tasks seem to be more along the lines of prompts (e.g., "discuss with a partner," "create a flyer").

- Creating interpersonal communication tasks that resemble real-world use of the target language and are relatable to all students in the class might be somewhat paradoxical. For example, it may be relatable for students to organize a fundraiser in their community, but would they do so in the target language? In the same vein, how do we ensure that all learners would be able to relate to a context that necessitates the use of the target language (e.g., you are a tourist in Paris, and your partner is a tour guide)? Furthermore, some instructors might feel uncomfortable about asking learners to assume someone else's identity, particularly if it implies "acting" as someone from another culture.

- Given that novice learners are exclusively reactive (i.e., they depend on their interlocutor to carry the bulk of the conversation), it is reasonable to question the merits of having two novice learners perform an interpersonal communication task based on a relatively open prompt. They should either be provided a more structured task to complete, or they should engage in interpersonal communication with the instructor, which can be done in small groups (e.g., two or three students at a time).

- The way IPA rubrics are worded and points are awarded might inadvertently send the wrong message to the students. For instance, Adair-Hauck et al. (2013) state that "a high B corresponds to the rubric label Meets Expectations—Strong" (p. 19). If a student is sustaining performance at level, why would they not get an A? The authors clarify that students do not need to exceed expectations for all criteria to earn an A, but this approach to grading could make some students who are actually at level feel like they have fallen short. We will talk more about rubrics in the next section.

Despite these concerns, IPAs have many great qualities that can be adapted or emulated, even if your circumstances don't allow for you to follow IPA guidelines and protocols to the letter. Here are just a few:

- Focus on what students can do with the language, as opposed to what they can memorize. Regardless of the format you end up choosing to evaluate your students, it shouldn't be about how many words and rules taught in class they can remember.

- Design communicative tasks for learners to perform (i.e., purposeful interpretation and expression of meaning), and make them as relevant and relatable as possible to students' lives.
- Fully integrate assessment and instruction, not only by making sure that what you do in class adequately prepares students, but also by adjusting what you focus on in class based on your students' performance.
- Focus on cohesive content (e.g., thematic units), as opposed to textbook chapters or grammar structures.
- If grades or points are to be assigned, reward sustaining performance at level, based on realistic expectations that stem from having a firm grasp on both proficiency levels and the fundamentals of second language acquisition.

Considerations for Effective Rubrics

The wording and type of rubric we use to evaluate performance is indeed a crucial aspect of successful assessment practices that are aligned with instruction. Let's start by clarifying that rubrics can be used to assign grades, but not necessarily. In fact, rubrics can be very helpful to provide feedback on performance, without any sort of numeric value attached to them.

There are two types of rubrics, each of which has its pros and cons:

- **Holistic rubrics** essentially evaluate performance overall, and each level contains a general description or a list of characteristics. They can be very useful for looking at the big picture (i.e., to what extent are learners able to perform this task at the targeted level?) and moving away from discrete-point testing (i.e., how many answers did they get right, and how many did they get wrong?). Two things to avoid when constructing holistic rubrics are: lumping too many descriptors together and having too many levels with overlapping descriptors.
- **Analytic rubrics** provide a more fine-grained evaluation of performance by breaking down various aspects or components of it. For instance, an analytic rubric for an argumentative essay might look at the title, the introduction, the organization, the clarity of ideas, etc. Each criterion is then evaluated on a scale (e.g., excellent, good, fair, needs improvement). The advantage of an analytic rubric is that it provides more detailed information about the learners' performance, and some instructors prefer them because they can

focus on separate aspects at a time, as opposed to struggling with making a single decision as is the case with holistic rubrics. For analytic rubrics to be useful, each point for each criterion should be well-defined and not overlap. Furthermore, it should be possible to evaluate each criterion separately: Students should not be penalized twice, so to speak.

In both cases, descriptors should be concise, clear, and written in a way that is accessible to all stakeholders. If they are too vague, technical, or complex, they will not help either the learners or the instructors understand to what extent they are on track toward meeting their communicative goals. For instance, saying that a learner is able to "create with language" might seem perfectly understandable to trained ACTFL raters, but the vast majority of students will not know exactly what that means. Here's an alternative for a holistic rubric that might be clearer: "Student is generally able to communicate ideas related to personal or concrete topics (preferences, routines, etc.) in a series of simple sentences that are comprehensible to the teacher."

Equally important, the wording for the possible levels of performance should not make it seem like the highest level is unattainable (e.g., "exemplary"), and the lowest level should not sound like we are disappointed or discounting the learner's efforts (e.g., "unsatisfactory"). Earlier, we alluded to a potential issue with rubrics where the maximum score for a given criterion is assigned to performance that "exceeds expectations": Full credit shouldn't be reserved for a speaker of a higher level than what we have been aiming for. If the rubric is being used only to provide learners with feedback on their performance, but not to assign any type of numeric score, then we should indeed let learners know in what aspects their performance exceeds expectations. However, when it comes to grading, a strong performance at level should receive the highest score. Therefore, instead of "meeting or exceeding expectations," a better alternative for the wording of the rubric, in our opinion, would be something along the lines of:

- Fully sustained performance at level
- Minimally sustained performance at level
- Frequent but not sustained performance at level
- Emerging performance at level
- Little to no evidence of performance at level
- No attempt at performance

Last, but not least, even though "square" rubrics are the most common ones, there is no law against weighing each criterion differently. In fact, we would argue that in a well-thought-out rubric, the weight of each criterion should reflect its importance relative to other criteria within the context of the task. For example, let's say you are evaluating an interpersonal task where you have a conversation with your students, who are novice-high/intermediate-low learners. You want to assess whether they are able to ask questions, but you know you'll be asking the bulk of the questions, and therefore, your main focus might be on whether they can provide the info requested in a comprehensible way. You could, then, distribute the points as follows:

- Criterion 1: Comprehensibility (worth 5 points)
- Criterion 2: Ability to provide requested information (worth 5 points)
- Criterion 3: Text type (worth 3 points)
- Criterion 4: Ability to ask questions (worth 2 points)

Before ACTFL revokes our memberships, we should clarify that we are not saying that text type doesn't matter or that asking questions is not important. We are only saying that there is nothing wrong with thinking outside the "square rubrics" box.

Intercultural Communication Goals

So far, we've been focusing on goals for the three modes of communication, but the Can-Do Statements also include benchmarks and performance indicators for intercultural communication. These involve knowledge of cultural products and practices that aid in the understanding of cultural perspectives, all of which contribute to developing intercultural competence.

Let's pause a minute here to define some of these terms:

- **Cultural products** refer to tangible or intangible creations (e.g., foods, musical instruments, flags, clothes, etc.).
- **Cultural practices** refer to behaviors (e.g., greetings, ways of interacting with elders, asking someone out, punctuality, etc.)
- **Cultural perspectives** refer to views and values (e.g., religious beliefs, perceptions of gender roles, attitude toward authority figures, etc.)
- **Intercultural competence** involves not just cultural knowledge, but, perhaps more important, attitudes such as curiosity and respect, as well as critical-thinking skills, and it progresses "from personal level (attitude) to interpersonal/interactive level (outcomes)" (Deardorff, 2006, p. 254).

Although the 3 Ps (products, practices, and perspectives) are widely used, we should avoid falling back on a superficial presentation of culture, one where students observe it from afar, as if they were tourists taking pictures from a double-decker bus. In other words, we might inadvertently approach the 3 Ps as a list of observations to make about the *other* culture (i.e., "look at what *they* do!"). To further illustrate this point, let's dissect the cultural practice of singing the national anthem before a baseball game in the United States:

- **Products:** the flag, the lyrics, the instruments, sometimes fireworks, military symbols, color guard, etc.
- **Practices:** standing up, putting your hand on your chest, singing, clapping at the end, etc.
- **Perspectives:** patriotism, admiration of military personnel, ideologies surrounding American exceptionalism.

Without engaging in a more in-depth discussion or analysis, the 3 Ps listed above could potentially lead students to jump to conclusions and walk away with reinforced negative stereotypes (e.g., "Americans think they're better than everyone else," "Americans are aggressive and glorify war").

Furthermore, although knowledge *about* the target cultures is a good first step, intercultural communication, by definition, is multidirectional and involves both our own and other cultures. Therefore, students should have the opportunity to critically reflect on both cultures, and we should guide them to move past making shallow comparisons or subjective classifications (e.g., "normal," "weird," etc.). Crane (2016) offers several great examples for incorporating structured reflections in the language curriculum, including novice-level courses. Unlike more traditional journaling, structured reflections build on each other and provide guiding questions to "help students make connections between their previously held assumptions, theories and concepts learned, and experiences beyond the classroom" (Crane, 2016, p. 53). Last, but not least, even though culture certainly has a collective aspect, it is important to include individual voices and stories to combat stereotypes.

In case you're wondering . . .

How do you have such complex discussions in the target language with novice-level learners? The simplest answer is: These discussions don't have to be in the target language! We advocate for maximizing target language use, but it is also important to foster intercultural competence, even with novice-level learners. We shouldn't treat culture superficially simply because students don't have the linguistic abilities to engage in structured reflections and in-depth discussions in the target language. Resorting to oversimplified observations could have more cons than pros. Just because some assignments do not require the use of the target language, that doesn't mean learning isn't happening.

Although the main focus of this book is language acquisition, we would be remiss if we did not acknowledge that acquiring a language is not synonymous with developing intercultural communication skills. Being able to communicate in the target language is an important part of intercultural competence, but there is much more to it. As educators, we should make a conscious effort to go beyond cultural knowledge and help students develop the skills and attitudes that encompass intercultural competence.

Many wonderful resources are dedicated entirely to fostering intercultural communicative competence, and we cannot possibly do this topic justice by simplifying and condensing it into one subsection. That being said, we want you to keep in mind a few key points, particularly as you plan your units and daily lessons:

- Avoid depicting culture as a side note, usually reduced to statistics and oddities (e.g., doing things like "Culture Fridays" or merely assigning students to do presentations on various countries). This approach could lead to erroneous generalizations and cultural stereotyping that do more harm than good. And, on a related note, avoid reinforcing associations between nationalities (countries) and cultures. One country does not equal one culture.

- Strive to integrate language and culture through authentic resources, individual narratives, and culturally relevant information. At the same time, it is OK to have some activities focused mainly on developing communicative ability or having fun with the language, and other activities where learners engage in more complex discussions and reflections without using the target language.

- Intercultural competence develops over time and through multiple experiences. Expecting learners to develop intercultural competence by watching publisher-provided cultural videos or learning fun facts about cultural products and practices is akin to expecting learners to develop language proficiency by watching grammar tutorials or memorizing vocab lists.

In a nutshell

Before we move on to classroom examples, summarize five main points from this chapter. What are your own takeaways?

_____

_____

_____

_____

_____

Would you like to learn more?
Go to **www.hackettpublishing.com/common-ground-resources**
for a list of suggested readings, webinars, and other resources.

WHAT DOES IT LOOK LIKE IN THE CLASSROOM?

Example 1: Thematic Unit for Novice Level

This example describes a unit with activities grouped by mode of communication to show the variety of ways in which learners engage with content, how the activities build on each other, and the ratio of activities for each mode. While the unit should certainly start with interpretive activities, the way we have grouped the activities does not represent the order in which they would happen in class. For instance, the teacher could do some interpretive activities, then one of the interpersonal activities followed by its corresponding presentational activity, and then continue with a few more interpretive activities, and so on.

Proficiency level: Novice-high

Thematic Unit: Self-Care and Healthy Habits

Can-Do Statements:

- I can read an infographic and understand major recommendations for healthy living.
- I can ask and answer simple questions about my health-related habits.
- I can determine how similar or different my habits are from other people's habits.
- I can make a list of healthy or unhealthy habits.

In-Class Activities: Interpretive

- **Activity 1:** The teacher describes their own routine and health-related habits, using visuals and gestures to aid comprehension and checking for comprehension through binary-choice questions and true/false items (described in Example 2 of Chapter 3).
- **Activity 2:** The teacher presents national statistics of various health-related habits (hours of sleep, caffeine consumption, etc.) and asks students binary-choice questions comparing the teacher's own habits and the national statistics.
- **Activity 3:** The teacher shows students an infographic about health-related habits in a country where the target language is spoken. Some keywords and phrases in the infographic have been

removed. The teacher provides a list of potential words and phrases, and the students need to reconstruct the infographic by selecting the right spot for each phrase. The keywords can have the translation or a clear image that supports understanding of these new words. This activity is meant to help students with comprehension and keyword recognition.

- **Activity 4:** Students are tasked with writing a summary (in the shared language) of the information contained in the infographic, in paragraph form. However, they need to leave some words out (on purpose!). They can write, for example: In (country), _____ % of people get _____ hours of sleep; _____ % try to avoid _____. Then, students exchange their summaries with someone else. They read what their classmate wrote and complete the blanks with the appropriate words based on the information in the infographic. Lastly, they return the summary to their classmate, who then verifies the answers. This activity is an additional way of working on identification of main ideas and keyword recognition.

- **Activity 5:** Students answer questions about how the trends in the two countries compare (to be answered in the shared language or partly in the target language, with the help of sentence starters). Some questions could be:
  ◦ What are two similar trends in both countries?
  ◦ What are two differences between the two countries?

- **Activity 6:** Students watch a video of two people describing their health-related habits in the target language. After watching each video, students classify the activities mentioned into healthy and unhealthy. Then, they are guided to establish comparisons between the two people, between the people in the video and the statistics they discussed, and between the people in the video and their own habits. Students complete this chart for each person in the video; then, they can use this information to establish connections:

Eating habits:	
Sleeping habits:	
Other habits:	
Similarities and differences with my own habits:	The person in the video . . . and I also . . . The person in the video . . . but I . . .

- **Activity 7**: After watching the videos, students play a true-or-false game. Students break into pairs, and each set of pairs has a sticky note placed between them. The teacher reads true/false sentences about the video. The goal is for the students to grab the sticky note only if the sentence is true. When a student has the sticky note and the sentence is true, that student earns a point. If the teacher reads a false statement, the students should leave the sticky note alone. However, if one student grabs it when the statement is false, their partner earns two points. If the statement is false, the class revisits the text and corrects the statement. At the end, students tally up the total points they won, and the teacher awards the winning student of each pair a small prize, such as stickers, chocolates, or pencils.

In-Class Activities: Interpersonal

- **Activity 1:** The teacher guides a discussion in the target language about how the students' habits compare to the national statistics (interpretive activity #2). The teacher starts with some binary-choice questions (e.g., do you sleep more or fewer hours?) and then expands the conversation through follow-up questions (e.g., how many hours do you sleep?). Questions inquire about habits of specific students, as well as the class as a whole. Students should pay attention to the information being shared since they will need it to complete one of the presentational activities later. This activity helps students not only to prepare for the interpersonal portion of the IPA (where the teacher will be interviewing students about their habits) but also to establish comparisons.

- **Activity 2:** Students survey their peers about their health-related habits using a chart similar to the one below. Students can create their own questions to ask their peers and brainstorm before the interview.

Question:	Student answer #1	Student answer #2	Student answer #3
Do you wake up early or late?			
(add your own)			
(add your own)			
(add your own)			
(add your own)			
(add your own)			

Then, students report on how their own habits compare to their class-mates' habits, and the teacher guides students in a discussion about which healthy habits they consider most important to maintain (if it's some-thing they already do) or to implement (if it's something they don't do).

In-Class Activities: Presentational

- **Activity 1:** The teacher and students co-construct a paragraph together based on class discussion (interpersonal activity #1). The teacher writes the paragraph on the board or projects it while typing. First, the teacher provides some sentence starters, such as the following:
  - "The infographic suggests that . . ."
  - "In our class, we . . ."
  - "One difference between the national statistics and our class is . . ."
  - "One trend from the national statistics that is true for our class is . . ."
  Students offer suggestions for completing the sentences. Gradually, the teacher encourages students to add additional sentences on their own by prompting them to include more detailed information (e.g., how many hours they sleep versus how many hours other classmates sleep).
- **Activity 2:** Students write a summary of the information gathered from the survey (interpersonal activity #2) plus the class discussion. The teacher collects the summaries, as well as the completed charts from the interpersonal activity. Each student receives a summary and a chart (originally from different students), and then they circulate around the room to find the summary and chart that match the ones they have.

Example 2: Adapted IPA and Rubrics for Novice Level

This example shows an adapted IPA that corresponds with the unit on healthy habits. It is adapted because it does not include all the usual questions you might see in the interpretive section of an IPA, and the interpersonal component has also been modified to include the instructor since novice learners are not yet able to carry out a conversation on their own. Immediately after each portion of the IPA, we provide the rubrics that correspond with it. The rubrics have also been modi-fied, although they are still based on ACTFL (2012a) Proficiency Guidelines. A student who can sustain the targeted level should earn 100%.

Level: Novice-high

Task overview: The principal at ABC school has noticed that the number of students missing classes due to illness has increased significantly in the last few months. She is concerned that students are neglecting their health and self-care. She wants to develop a campaign of public service announcements created by students to address this issue. The announcements should shed light on a particular unhealthy habit, and they should include suggestions for the students and school to help address this problem.

Interpretive Task

The text is an infographic about healthy habits from a country where the target language is spoken. This infographic should be different from the one students have seen in class.

Part 1: Keyword recognition

- Students are given a list of words in the shared language, and they need to find the target-language equivalent within the text of the infographic. The words selected should be relatively important to the understanding of the text.

Part 2: Main ideas and supporting details

- The teacher provides students with a summary of the information in the shared language in paragraph form, but some of the details do not match what the infographic says; students have to spot the differences and correct the paragraph based on the information in the infographic.
- The students also answer other comprehension questions (in the shared language or a mix of the target and shared languages), such as:
  - Of the healthy eating habits mentioned in the infographic, which one do you think is the most important? And why do you feel that one is more important than the others?
- What are two effects of bad health habits?

Part 3: Inferences (to be answered in the shared language or partly in the target language)

- What age group is the intended audience of this infographic? And what makes you think that?
- What would be some additional information that could be added to one of the tips mentioned in the infographic?

Part 4: Cultural perspectives (to be answered in the shared language)

- How do these suggestions compare with those that we typically make in our country?

- What could explain some of the similarities and differences between the suggestions in the infographic and those that we typically make in our country?

Part 5: Compare and contrast (to be answered in the shared language or partly in the target language, with the help of sentence starters)

- Students are provided with a copy of the infographic they have discussed in class, and they are asked to list:
  - Similarities between the ideas and information in both infographics
  - Contrasts or differing information between the two infographics
  - Information included in one of the infographics, but not the other

Rubric for the Interpretive Task

Criterion 1 (worth 4 points): Word recognition
1 = Student can identify a few of the keywords.
2 = Student can identify half of the keywords.
3 = Student can identify most of the keywords.
4 = Student can identify all of the keywords.

Criterion 2 (worth 4 points): Comprehension of main ideas
1 = Student can only identify one of the main ideas, but is not yet able to identify supporting details.
2 = Student can only identify a few of the main ideas and supporting details.
3 = Student can identify most of the main ideas and supporting details.
4 = Student can identify all of the main ideas and supporting details.

Criterion 3 (worth 4 points): Interpretation beyond main ideas
1 = Student is not yet able to answer inference and cultural perspective questions; responses do not make sense for the given text.
2 = Student can partially answer inference and cultural perspective questions; some of the responses may not make sense for the given text.
3 = Student can answer most of the inference and cultural perspective questions; some ideas may need further development or support.
4 = Student can accurately and fully answer inference and cultural perspective questions.

Criterion 4 (worth 4 points): Compare and contrast
1 = Student is not yet able to establish clear connections and comparisons between the infographics.
2 = Student can state a few facts from the infographics that are vaguely related or connected.
3 = Student can partially state some similarities and contrasts between the infographics.
4 = Student can clearly state several similarities and differences between the infographics.

Interpersonal Task

The teacher meets with two students at a time, playing the role of a school principal who is concerned with the self-care habits of the students. The purpose of the conversation is to better understand what issues students struggle with, what their health-related habits are, and what the school can do to help them. The conversation starts by establishing a connection with the information the students learned in the interpretive portion. The students can have a copy of the text with them. Some questions could include:

- Based on the infographic in the interpretive section, how good are your health-related habits?
- Which health-related habits mentioned in the infographic do you consider most important?
- What are some positive health-related habits you have?
- What is one health-related habit you want to change or improve?
- What are some negative health-related habits that some students in our school have?
- What consequences or effects do these issues have for students?
- What changes can students make to improve their health?

The teacher can modify the questions to make them more comprehensible, as needed. The teacher should also ask follow-up questions on what students are sharing (e.g., if a student says they don't sleep well, the teacher can ask "how many hours do you sleep?", "what time do you go to bed?", "do you watch TV or use your phone right before you go to bed?", etc.).

Rubric for the Interpersonal Task
Criterion 1 (worth 4 points): Text type
1 = Most responses consist of one or two isolated words.
2 = Most responses consist of a few words.
3 = Most responses consist of a few words and some memorized chunks/phrases.
4 = Most responses consist of a mixture of words, phrases, and occasional simple sentences.

Criterion 2 (worth 4 points): Comprehensibility
1 = All utterances are very difficult to understand, even by a very sympathetic interlocutor.
2 = Most utterances are difficult to understand, even by a sympathetic interlocutor.
3 = Some utterances are difficult to understand, even by a sympathetic interlocutor.
4 = Most utterances are generally comprehensible to a sympathetic interlocutor, although communication breakdowns occur from time to time.

Criterion 3 (worth 4 points): Ability to provide requested information
1 = Student is unable to understand the questions and rarely provides the requested information.
2 = Student is able to understand only a few of the questions; most responses are off topic.
3 = Student is able to understand about half of the questions; some responses are off topic.
4 = Student is able to understand most of the questions and responses are generally on topic.

Presentational Task

Using the information students learned in the interpretive and interpersonal sections of the IPA, they create a public service announcement video to raise awareness of an unhealthy habit students may have and what they can do to overcome it and improve their health. Their announcement should explain why this issue is important (i.e., what consequences it can have), and it should include recommendations of concrete steps that students can take, as well as suggestions for the school to help students. Students should get started on this task in class and then finalize it outside of class. This way, students have adequate time to complete the task, and the teacher can ensure that everyone is on the right track, while also discouraging the use of unauthorized assistance (e.g., online translators).

Rubric for the Presentational Task
Criterion 1 (worth 4 points): Information provided
1 = Very few of the required information is included, and all sections need significantly more development.
2 = Only some of the required information is included, and most sections lack details and need more development.
3 = Most of the required information is included, but some sections lack details and need more development.
4 = All of the required information is included, with specific details addressing the prompt.

Criterion 2 (worth 4 points): Organization and visual support
1 = The presentation is generally hard to follow and lacks relevant visual aids.
2 = Content is presented in a somewhat clear way, although at times, it is hard to follow, with only a few relevant visual aids.
3 = Content is presented in a generally clear way, with mostly relevant visual aids.
4 = Content is presented in a clear way, with relevant visual aids.

Criterion 3 (worth 4 points): Voice narration in the target language

1 = All utterances are very difficult to understand, even by a very sympathetic interlocutor, except for a few isolated words.

2 = Narration consists of sentence fragments that are generally difficult to understand, even by a sympathetic interlocutor.

3 = Narration consists of a mixture of sentence fragments and words that are somewhat comprehensible to a sympathetic interlocutor.

4 = Narration consists of mostly simple sentences that are generally comprehensible to a sympathetic interlocutor.

Example 3: Thematic Unit for Intermediate/Advanced Level

Similar to the thematic unit presented earlier, this example lists the activities related to the topic of current events, grouped by mode. Once again, the unit should start with interpretive activities, but the way in which we have listed the activities here does not necessarily represent the order in which they would happen in class. Many of the activities in this thematic unit are developed in detail in subsequent chapters. Our main goal here is to give you an idea of how you could incorporate those ideas into a unit.

Proficiency level: Intermediate-high/advanced-low

Can-Do Statements:

- I can understand the main events and actions related to social justice issues in a specific country.
- I can describe and explain current events and social justice issues in my community.
- I can exchange information and ideas about current events and social justice issues.

In-Class Activities: Interpretive

- **Activity 1:** Students read a newspaper article describing a protest that took place in a country where the target language is spoken. The pre- and post-reading activities are developed in Example 5 of Chapter 4.
- **Activity 2:** Students watch a news broadcast from the same country that explains more about the protests the article describes. The teacher plays the broadcast a few times; students complete a Venn

diagram summarizing the information that was mentioned only in the broadcast, only in the article, or in both. Students compare their Venn diagrams in small groups and add any details they are missing.

- **Activity 3:** Using the information they gained from the article and the broadcast, students work in pairs to write a tweet retelling the event, but each pair is secretly assigned a number of inaccurate details they need to include: Some pairs get 0 (i.e., nothing should be inaccurate), while others get 1, 2, or 3. Once students have written their tweets, they post them in an online forum, or they can post the tweets around the classroom. Their classmates read the tweets and indicate if they are "fake news" or not, and they fact-check the information (i.e., correct what is inaccurate), if needed.

- **Activity 4:** Students create an artistic collage or mini-mural representing their interpretation of the protests and the social cause behind it. They can, then, complete a gallery walk (also explained in Example 5 of Chapter 4).

In-Class Activities: Interpersonal

- **Activity 1:** Students interact in small groups, discussing connections between the event in the article and the broadcast and other current events in their community or other countries. Students also brainstorm questions they would ask someone who lives in the country where the protests took place (to be used in Activity 2).

- **Activity 2:** Students interview a speaker of the target language through a video-chat platform to find out what is happening where that person lives and their opinions on the protests. If it is not possible for all students to interact with someone from the country where the protests took place, students could connect with someone from a different country and learn about similar events elsewhere. The interviews should be recorded since students will need the information for one of the presentational tasks.

In-Class Activities: Presentational

- **Activity 1:** Students write a reflection after completing the gallery walk (see Example 5 of Chapter 4).

- **Activity 2:** Students work in pairs to create a video newscast where they summarize the information they learned in the interpretive activities, as well as new information they learned through their video-chat interview.

Example 4: Adapted IPA for Intermediate/Advanced Level

This example shows an adapted IPA that corresponds with the unit on current events and social justice described in Example 3. It is adapted because it does not include all the traditional questions you might see in the interpretive section of an IPA.

Proficiency level: Intermediate-high/advanced-low

Task overview: Social justice issues like the ones we have been exploring in class are prevalent in all communities, including ours. As we have learned, people can do a lot to raise awareness and effect change. Now it is your turn to plan an event that would bring attention to a social cause in our community. You will first learn about the details of an event from the perspective of the activist who organized it, and then you will work with a classmate to plan your own event to take place at our school. Finally, you will write an email to inform the principal of your idea and persuade them to support your event.

Interpretive Task

You will watch a video of an interview with an activist who helped organize protests related to the social issues we have been discussing in class. You will watch the video twice, and you can take notes as you watch.

Part 1: Main ideas and supporting details

- Students write a paragraph in the target language, summarizing the content of the interview.
- Students provide a list of relevant tags they would include for this video so others could find the video online.
- Students also answer other comprehension questions (in the target language), such as:
  - What motivated the activist to organize this event?
  - What are some challenges the activist had to overcome while organizing this event?
  - What are some similarities and differences between the event the activist describes in this video and the protests we learned about in class?

Part 2: Inference questions (to be answered in the shared language or a mix of the target and shared languages)

- What would you say are other causes that this activist might support? And why?
- What are some short-term and long-term changes that could arise because of the protest organized by the activist in the video?

Part 3: Cultural perspectives questions (to be answered in the shared language or a mix of the target and shared languages)

- How does the protest organized by the activist in the video compare with those that we typically have in our country? And what could explain some of those similarities and differences?
- What do you think would be the reaction of different groups in our community if that event were organized here?

Interpersonal Task

Keeping in mind the information shared by the activist in the video and what we have learned in class regarding social protests, you will plan your own event. In small groups, discuss what social causes you feel deserve more attention in our community, and what are the best ways to raise awareness and ignite change by motivating others to become involved. Also discuss possible challenges, as well as what you will need to do for the event to be successful.

By the end of your discussion, you should have decided the following:

- What social justice cause (only one!) you want to focus on, and why it is important to bring attention to this cause.
- The type of event you feel would be most effective to bring attention to the cause. Plan your event in detail (i.e., when, where, etc.), including how you will spread the word about it.
- What you will need to organize the event and make it a success (e.g., posters, volunteers, megaphones, social media posts, etc.).

Presentational Task

Now that you have a concrete plan, you need permission to host your event at our school. Write an email to the principal to explain your idea and convince them of the importance of your event. Be sure to include the following:

- The social cause you chose to focus on, and why it is important
- The details of your event (i.e., what, when, where, who)

- The steps you are taking to organize it
- How the event will benefit our community

Example 5: Activity on Products, Practices, and Perspectives

This example describes an activity to discuss cultural products, practices, and perspectives—the 3 Ps—with your students. Although the activity starts at the observation level by asking students to list examples, the main focus is on thinking critically about "culture" as a concept. Note that the focus is not necessarily the target cultures; in fact, the examples should be from any cultures that the students are familiar with. Depending on the proficiency level of your students, most of this activity may need to be done in the shared language, as opposed to the target language.

Proficiency level: Varied

Step 1: The teacher gives students a handout with a definition of each of the 3 Ps in the target language. Then, the teacher shows a list with a few examples of each category (e.g., "shaking hands when meeting someone for the first time"), and students work in small groups to classify the examples. When they have finished, the teacher displays the answers, and the class discusses any discrepancies.

Step 2: The class is divided into two teams, and they each have their own section of the board where they will write new examples as a relay race. Each student should write an example for any of the three categories, whichever they can think of first, but they cannot copy an example from the other team. They have five minutes to suggest as many examples as possible. The examples can be related to any culture students are familiar with. The team who wins has the longest list of total examples.

Step 3: The teacher leads a discussion based on the following questions:

- Which category had the longest list of examples? Why do you think it was easier to think of examples for that category?
- Which category had the fewest examples? Why do you think it was harder to think of examples for that category?
- What implications does that have for how we define or perceive "culture"? Do we tend to focus more on the visible or superficial part of culture more than the invisible or intangible aspects of culture?
- Are there some examples that fit into multiple categories? What are the intersections?
- Which examples could be perceived as stereotypical?
- What are some stereotypes associated with these examples?
- What are some consequences of negative stereotypes?

Now That You Know

Discussion and Expansion Questions

1) Why do you think the Can-Do Statements are written from the learners' point of view ("I can . . .")? What are the benefits of involving learners in understanding their abilities in the target language and where they are in their proficiency journey? Would you—or do you—discuss some basic aspects of language acquisition with your students? Why or why not?

2) Even though the Can-Do Statements are written in first person, some people argue that they don't sound like something a learner would say. Do you think the language of the Can-Do Statements is accessible to learners? In other words, if you asked your students to read them, would they understand what each statement refers to? And would you have your students reflect on what they are able and not yet able to do in the target language, using the Can-Do Statements?

3) Read the complete ACTFL (2012a) Proficiency Guidelines (available online), and then answer the following questions:
   a) What keywords would you choose to summarize each of the major proficiency levels? Create a word cloud for each one.
   b) Are there any words or phrases in the guidelines that could be problematic? How would you rephrase them?

4) Evaluate the following goals, which could be for lessons, units, or activities, especially with respect to whether they're measurable and focus on communication:

   Students will be able to . . .

   . . . practice expressing likes and dislikes.

   . . . learn adjectives used to describe clothing.

   . . . gain an appreciation for different ways of greeting someone.

   . . . describe the neighborhood where they live.

   . . . use future tense to make predictions about their lives in 20 years.

   . . . express doubts using the subjunctive.

   . . . practice asking and answering questions.

   . . . indicate the location of objects in a room.

   . . . understand an authentic TV commercial.

5) Since the way we assess proficiency is based on exams that tend to follow a certain protocol because they need to be valid and reliable, we could argue that test takers can prepare and rehearse similar tasks. In that case, are we truly measuring proficiency, or is it still performance? For instance, if you search online, you will find sites that offer courses or modules to prepare to take the Oral Proficiency Interview (OPI). So, can we ever really measure what someone can do with the language in a spontaneous, real-world context?

6) Consider the following scenario of misalignment between instruction and assessment, and complete the last sentence:

> In class, students learn rules, do a lot of mechanical practice (worksheets with fill-in-the-blanks), and play games to help them memorize the chapter vocab; tests include interpretive, inter-personal, and presentational tasks. This scenario usually leads to _____ on the part of the instructor, and _____ on the part of the students.

7) In your experience as a student in a language course, how was "culture" approached? Would you say intercultural competence was fostered in class?

8) Following the example of singing the anthem at sporting events that we discussed in this chapter, propose another example that illustrates the connection between the 3 Ps (products, practices, and perspectives) for a culture associated with the language you teach. Then, reflect on potential misinterpretations, generalizations, or stereotypes associated with your example, particularly with respect to perspectives.

9) In this chapter, we hinted at the fact that, ideally, there should be a balance when it comes to topics: some should be proposed by the students, and others should be selected by the instructor. Which topics are your students likely to suggest, and which topics would you consider important to include, even if they are not among your students' suggestions?

10) What do you think about the following rubric for a novice-high/intermediate-low presentational writing task? Read the wording of each description carefully, and think about the characteristics of good rubrics we discussed in this chapter. What would you leave as is, and what would you revise, and why?

Point values	4 points	3 points	2 points	1 point
Task completion	Student's response addresses all parts of the prompt and includes well-developed ideas and supporting details.	Student addresses all parts of the prompt, but there is very little elaboration or details.	Student addresses some of the prompt, but not all of it. Ideas lack development and details.	Student does not address most parts of the prompt; ideas are repetitive and/or unrelated to the task.
Comprehensibility	The reader can easily understand the message; brief pauses may be needed to figure out a phrase or two.	The reader may need to figure out a few phrases throughout the writing.	The reader can figure out about half of the text, but significant parts are difficult to understand.	The reader can figure out little to none of the writing because the text is almost impossible to understand.
Discourse and organization	Student is frequently combining sentences using connecting words. Writing is sequenced logically.	Student is starting to combine sentences. Writing is sequenced logically, for the most part.	Student writes predominantly complete sentences, but writing demonstrates little organization.	Student writes in some sentences and some phrases. Writing has little to no organization.
Lexical variety	Student uses vocabulary from a variety of units covered in the course. Almost all the vocabulary is used accurately.	Student uses some vocabulary from a variety of units covered in the course, but very few words come from the current unit. Most of the vocabulary is used accurately.	Student uses a limited amount of vocabulary from previous topics, but much of it is repetitive. Almost half of the vocabulary is used incorrectly.	Student repeats most of the vocabulary used. Less than half of the vocabulary is used accurately.
Language control	Student demonstrates consistent control of all grammar concepts studied in the course up to that point.	Student demonstrates partial control of most grammar concepts studied in the course up to that point.	Student demonstrates control of only a few grammar concepts studied in the course up to that point.	Student demonstrates little to no control of any of the grammar concepts studied in the course up to that point.

11) Earlier in this chapter, we said that we tend to think of grades as a reflection of how well students were able to meet the instructional goals or reach the intended level. Do you agree with that statement? Is there a correlation between grades and the students' proficiency level or abilities in the target language? What does an "A" mean in your course?

12) Some educators prefer holistic rubrics when evaluating interpersonal communication because it is indeed more difficult to evaluate specific aspects of the interaction separately, particularly when it is not recorded, and even more so when the instructor is one of the interlocutors. How would you transform the analytic rubric for the interpersonal mode in Example 2 into a holistic rubric?

13) What do you think about the following idea for an adapted IPA? What level would you say it is targeting? Would you change or adapt anything if you were to use it in one of your classes?

> **Task overview:** Experts say that watching TV shows and movies in another language can indeed be very beneficial for language learning, but the key is to be really interested in understanding what's going on. In other words, it needs to be binge-worthy! You will be working in teams to create a new TV series that would be appealing to students like you.
>
> **Interpretive:** Students read a blog post about characteristics of good TV shows ("10 Key Elements to Any Good TV Show"), and they evaluate a sample pitch based on what they now know about aspects of successful TV shows.
>
> **Interpersonal:** Students discuss their TV-viewing habits and preferences, comparing them to what the article said about elements of successful TV shows. They also brainstorm ideas for their own pitch.
>
> **Presentational:** Students create a TV series pitch, combining the elements and preferences they learned about in the interpretive and the interpersonal phases. They present the pitch to their classmates, and the class votes for their favorite.

Observation and Application Activities

1) Search for rubrics online, particularly those targeting the interpersonal mode, and answer the following questions:

   a) Are they holistic or analytic?

   b) To what extent do they represent good examples, based on the guidelines discussed in this chapter?

    c) What would you need to modify if you were going to use them for a higher or lower level?

2) Observe an introductory- or intermediate-level class of the language you teach. Take notes on the following:

    a) What Can-Do Statements guided the lesson, if any?

    b) What formative assessments did you observe? Remember that formative assessments don't necessarily have a grade attached.

    c) How was "culture" integrated? If it wasn't, suggest ways in which it could have been.

3) Create an adapted IPA for the language and level you teach that would be appropriate for a thematic unit on animals/pets, which can be approached from many different angles, depending on your students' age and their proficiency level. Remember to create a task overview, as well as interpretive, presentational, and interpersonal tasks.

Section II

Interpretive Communication

Chapter 3
Input

WHAT DO I NEED TO KNOW?

Characteristics of Input

"Input" is another extremely important term to define. Input that contributes to acquisition is essentially the target language that is being processed for meaning. Note that we are not saying "language that the learner is exposed to" because input that is actually helpful for acquisition is much more than exposure: If learners are not understanding, then they cannot make form-meaning connections, and thus, they're not building a linguistic system in their heads that they can use for communicative purposes.

In a typical classroom, learners are exposed to the target language in various ways, but not all of these ways contribute to language acquisition. Consider the following examples, paying close attention to the differences between the ones that count as input for acquisition and those that do not.

What counts as input	What doesn't count as input
Students are given 10 steps to a recipe, but in the wrong order. They are told to put the sentences in the right order and finally guess what dish the recipe is for.	Students are told to read a dialogue between a waiter and a customer. Then, they act it out in front of the class.
The teacher says (in the target language): "Get up." Students get up.	The teacher shows students examples of formal and informal commands.
The teacher describes what their house looks like and shows students three pictures of different houses. Students select the picture that matches the description.	The teacher describes what they did last weekend. Students look confused, so the teacher translates everything into the shared language.
The teacher gives students a map of a town, tells them where they are, and gives them directions (e.g., "Turn left on Main Street"). Students indicate on the map the route and the destination.	The teacher plays a song and gives students the lyrics, but with some words missing. Students fill in the blanks with the right words while they listen to the song.
The teacher gives students the menus for four different restaurants. Students choose the best one for someone who is a vegetarian, someone on a tight budget, and someone looking to take their significant other on a romantic date.	Students match a list of conjugated verbs with their corresponding infinitive forms.

All of the scenarios in the second column (what doesn't count) could be done without the students even attempting to extract meaning from the target language. They can read a dialogue without understanding what they're saying. They can listen to a song, recognize sounds, and fill in the blanks without understanding most of the lyrics. However, to complete all of the tasks in the first column (what counts), students need to understand the *meaning* of the message.

In sum, students should be **able and compelled to understand** the target language. Does that mean that students need to understand every single word, or that the input must be tailored to each student's interests? That's what we will discuss in this chapter. Let's start by defining "comprehensible input" and exploring how we can help make the input comprehensible. Later, we will tackle the issue of compelling learners to understand the input.

The (Comprehensible) Input Hypothesis

In the 1980s, Stephen Krashen proposed the Input Hypothesis, which is probably the most influential of the five hypotheses that made up his Monitor Model.

This hypothesis basically defines what learners need to acquire a language: input that is comprehensible and that contains "structures that are a bit beyond our own level of competence" (Krashen, 1985, p. 2). Even though Krashen's ideas have been criticized, everyone agrees that input is *necessary*: without input, and without understanding the input, there is no acquisition. Whether it is *sufficient* or not (i.e., all you need is input) is something we will address in another chapter.

Now, the part about the precise level of input needed ("a bit beyond" our current level) is easier said than done, and that's one of the criticisms of Krashen's Input Hypothesis. How do we know what a student's current level of competence is, and how do we know exactly what is "a bit beyond"? And is it even possible to apply that idea to a class of 20 or 30 students? Our advice would be not to obsess about achieving the perfect level of input (because it doesn't exist!), and instead aim for most of the input to be comprehensible, avoiding the two extremes:

- **Too difficult:** If the input is too difficult to comprehend without providing frequent translations, then it won't contribute much—if anything—toward acquisition. For example, if you only know "hello" and "please" in Russian, and you watch a Russian movie with English subtitles, chances are you will only process the English subtitles and not acquire any Russian at all.

- **Too easy:** If the input *never* contains *anything* new (i.e., you only use very simple sentences full of cognates that *all* your students can *fully* understand 100% of the time, and that's the only target language they are ever exposed to), the input will be comprehensible, but learners' linguistic system won't develop or expand. Our goal as input providers should not be for students to understand every word, every time. In fact, we should help learners feel comfortable with not understanding every word!

And remember: You are not a machine, and neither are your students! You cannot predict precisely what they will and will not understand. The takeaway is to be mindful of the extent to which they will be able to understand so you can consider ways to make the input more comprehensible without frequent translations. That way, learners can demonstrate comprehension through tasks that are indeed doable for their level.

Sources of Input

Now that we've established what we mean by comprehensible input, let's look at how we can provide it for our students. In a classroom context, there are several sources of input:

- The teacher
- Resources made for language learners
- Authentic resources
- Other students

Let's put the input from other students aside for now; we will come back to that idea when we talk about output and interaction. Here, we will discuss the other three main sources of input.

The Teacher

The teacher is one of the most important sources of input for learners. Class time might be the only time learners engage in meaningful comprehension of the target language, so it is crucial for the instructor to maximize its use. However, we are not saying you should use the target language regardless of whether your students can understand you or not. If they're not understanding, it's just noise, and it doesn't count as input for acquisition. In fact, students are bound to get frustrated because they cannot understand anything, and that will only make matters worse. What we are saying is that you should use precious class time wisely by providing *comprehensible* input as much as possible from day 1.

Staying in the target language without resorting to frequent translations can be challenging, particularly with novice-level learners, but it is certainly not impossible. First and foremost, make sure that the topic and text type are appropriate for the students' proficiency level, following what we discussed in Chapter 2. Then, use one or more of the following strategies to help learners understand without translating for them:

- **Using visual cues:** pictures, drawings, charts, objects in the classroom, etc.
  - Make sure the images provide a clear representation of what you are trying to say, without room for misinterpretation.
  - Avoid pointing to students to demonstrate the meaning of words (e.g., "long hair," "blue shirt"), as some might be uncomfortable being the center of attention.

- **Using body language:** acting things out, making gestures, modeling instructions (i.e., pretend you are doing the activity), etc.
  - Be aware of the appropriateness or the meaning of certain gestures in different cultures because there could be misunderstandings.

- **Using target-language equivalents:** paraphrasing, defining in very simple terms, using a synonym, using related words (e.g., the verb "to work" and the adjective "hardworking").
  - Avoid definitions that are too long or convoluted; most times, if you can't define it in one simple sentence, it's probably best to use a different strategy or provide the translation.

- **Using examples and common associations:** brands, places, famous people, etc.
  - Be aware of references that your students will understand.
  - Avoid inadvertently putting anyone on the spot for not being familiar with a product or celebrity.

- **Using cognates:** if possible, use words that "look" and/or "sound" very similar in both languages and mean the same thing, provided they are appropriate for the context.
  - Some cognates are more easily recognizable in writing as opposed to spoken language. Even if, for you, it is quite obvious that the word is a cognate, it might be helpful to display it in written form so learners can read it.

- **Slowing down and simplifying:** speaking more slowly, adding emphasis to certain words, articulating words clearly, including pauses to give learners more processing time, using shorter and simpler utterances, repeating or rephrasing with synonyms, etc.
  - Simplifying doesn't mean sacrificing the grammaticality of what you're saying (e.g., "me very sad") or using words that would sound unnatural in the target language (e.g., cognates that might mean the same but are not used in the same contexts).

In case you're wondering . . .

What if none of the strategies seem to be working? We won't deny that some words are difficult to define, act out, or draw, and they might not have any suitable synonyms. In those cases, a quick translation can be an effective way to facilitate comprehension. However, it could also be a slippery slope. If you routinely translate to make sure learners understood, some students might eventually stop making an effort to pay attention to the target language for meaning, which is precisely what drives acquisition. Try to keep it in the target language as much as possible. And it doesn't hurt to remind students that they don't need to know the exact translation of every word you are saying.

Resources Made for Language Learners

Examples of materials made for learners that count as great sources of input are: short readings or novels (usually written by very creative language teachers), TV-series-type videos that follow carefully crafted scripts for specific proficiency levels, short videos describing an aspect of a community where the target language is spoken, etc.

The main advantage of these types of materials is that they're easier for learners to understand and for instructors to use in the classroom. The fact that learners are able to understand them with little scaffolding can give learners a confidence boost and motivate them to seek more meaningful input in the target language, which in turn will be extremely valuable in terms of acquisition. On the other hand, materials made for learners can be perceived as being more artificial or unnatural than "real" language use, and thus, some learners might not find them very engaging. However, saying that all resources made for learners are inauthentic (or fake) is an unfair characterization. There is nothing wrong with modifying the language to communicate genuine content. In fact, we do that all the time: Changing or simplifying our words to reach a specific audience is authentic language use.

Authentic Resources

Authentic resources are any type of materials (readings, videos, music, art, advertisements, social media posts, etc.) that have not been created for a language learner. For instance, a translation of an original work in another language could be an authentic resource if it was not created for language learners.

The pros and cons of authentic resources are basically the opposite of those of materials made for learners, which is an indication that both have a place in the language classroom. Authentic resources are a great way to make the language come alive: They provide rich content for learners, naturally integrate culture, and are often more engaging for students than teacher-made materials. Plus, being able to understand authentic resources can be a very rewarding accomplishment for learners, and thus, highly motivating for them to continue on their proficiency journey.

On the other hand, authentic resources have two drawbacks, both of which are related to the key qualities of input we mentioned at the beginning of the chapter: (1) they might be more difficult for learners to understand without proper scaffolding, and (2) since they don't come with accompanying activities, like resources made for learners, some teachers are unsure about what to do with them. Just showing students an ad or playing a song won't do much for acquisition if learners are not doing anything with the input. What can students do? The section "What does it look like in the classroom?" includes a couple of activity ideas using authentic resources, and Chapter 4 will include a few more.

One important point about authentic resources is that you can still incorporate them into your lessons even if they are not serving as a source of input. For example, there is a lot of value in playing a song and having learners list the instruments they hear or tell you if the song sounds like another song they know. They might end up liking the song so much that they want to listen to other songs by that artist in their spare time, and that might have a huge impact on both their motivation and their language development. On a related note, authentic resources don't always have to contain the target language. For example, a picture in a newspaper is also an authentic resource. Other examples of authentic materials that include hardly any language are: paintings, silent short films, comic strips without dialogue, instrumental music videos, certain promotional videos, movie posters, social media ads, etc.

Compelling Learners to Understand

At the beginning of this chapter, we mentioned the two key qualities of input, which boil down to the following: **learners should be both able and compelled to understand the target language for input to contribute to language acquisition.** As we saw, instructors can provide comprehensible input in many ways, but that only takes care of the first part: being able to understand. If learners are not being held accountable for understanding, you have no way of verifying that the input is being processed for meaning.

How can we **compel** them to understand? Learners are naturally compelled to understand input that is interesting to them, but it's unlikely that you will find a topic that everyone finds fascinating, and tailoring each class to the individual interests of 20+ students is impossible. Therefore, every time you provide comprehensible input, you should give students a clear reason for paying attention and understanding as much as possible. Ensuring that students are processing the target language for meaning is not just a strategy or a suggestion, but rather a key quality of the input we provide in class if our goal is language acquisition. Remember one of our key questions in Chapter 1: "What will others do with this information?"

Here are some general ideas of what learners can do with the input:

- Binary choice questions (e.g., true/false, me too/not me, good/bad, etc.)
- Putting in order
- Testing their memory (e.g., after looking at an image, watching a video, etc.)
- Guessing what/who (celebrities, places, etc.)
- Matching
- Voting/surveying (e.g., raise your hand if . . .)

- Ranking
- Inferring/drawing conclusions
- Indicating degree of probability, agreement, frequency, etc.
- Acting things out/moving
- Drawing/selecting images

If you go back to the table at the beginning of the chapter, where we listed what type of input contributes and doesn't contribute to language acquisition, you will notice that in all of the examples in the first column, there is an action or outcome that lets the instructor know whether students understood. There is a clear answer to the question: "What do the students need to do with this information?"

Now, let's revisit one of the examples from the second column of that table: "The teacher describes what they did last weekend." Imagine that the teacher implements our suggestions about how to make the message comprehensible (visuals, gestures, modified speech, etc.). As happy as we are to hear that this teacher is following our advice, there is still something very important missing: learners are **able** but not necessarily **compelled** to understand what the teacher is saying. It is unclear what students need to do with that information. If the teacher had shown them a series of pictures and asked them to choose which ones the teacher took based on the activities mentioned, then the learners would have had a clear purpose for the information and would have been compelled to understand.

Comprehension Checks

Making sure students are understanding is, of course, essential. Is it enough to ask students to raise their hand if they're not understanding? In an ideal world, that might be enough, but in the reality of the classroom, where some students might avoid admitting that they're lost in front of everyone, we need a different strategy. The best way to check for comprehension is by creating activities with a clear outcome or purpose that compels students to understand, as we explained in the preceding section.

Another way in which instructors often check for understanding is by asking display questions (i.e., questions that they know the answer to). For example, a teacher might show students a picture from a recent trip and ask students something like "Where is this? Is it a beach or the mountains?" That is the epitome of a display question: Of course the teacher knows the answer! The question has no purpose other than to verify understanding and maintain the learners' attention. These types of questions are not inherently bad. Teachers need a way to ensure that students are actively engaged in understanding the language, and it would be very difficult to do so if we couldn't ask any questions that we knew the answer to. The problem is when the sole purpose of an entire activity or lesson is "to learn food vocab," "to practice expressing likes and dislikes," or something along those lines.

Why does it matter? Without a communicative purpose, students won't be compelled to engage in communication, whether it is to understand or to express meaning. Would you feel compelled to continue paying attention after the 20th question with no purpose, and particularly when the question is not directed to you? If students know you're not going anywhere with your questions, and you're asking them just to "practice," they will likely tune out and stop processing the input for meaning, grinding acquisition to a halt.

In case you're wondering . . .

Is it better if we ask personal questions instead of display questions? Better is a relative term! If the teacher asks something like "Do you prefer cats or dogs?" and then moves on to something else, the purpose for asking that question remains unclear: It doesn't appear that the teacher will do anything with that information. However, questions like those can be a fantastic way to build rapport with your students. You get to know them, you connect with them—what's not to love? One thing you may want to consider is: How do we really know that students understood? They could just respond "dogs" because that's the last thing they heard. So, if possible, ask a simple follow-up question that might help you to ensure understanding, such as "what types of dogs do you like?"

The Role of Input

Now that you know exactly what we mean every time we say "input," let's talk about why it is absolutely necessary for language acquisition—and that's one thing nobody disputes in the entire field of SLA! Input is necessary because it gives learners the data needed to build a linguistic system, to put it simply. And nothing else gives them those building blocks.

What exactly do learners do with input? As learners understand what they're reading or listening to, they start making **form-meaning connections**. And yes, that goes for both "vocab" and "grammar." Let's look at some examples.

If I told you, totally out of context and without any visual cues, "I love my wugs," you would be confused, and your brain wouldn't be able to establish a connection between the form "wug" and its meaning. But if I said, "I love my wugs" and showed you a picture of two funny-looking birds, your brain would make a connection between the **form** "wug" and its **meaning**: a type of bird. Is one exposure enough? The short answer is no. Sometimes a word or object is so eye-catching that when you see or hear it once, you'll never forget its meaning, but for the most part, input doesn't work that way.

Now, let's see how learners get "grammar" from the input using the same example: "I love my wugs." How did you know I had more than one? The **form** "-s" attached to a noun in English is conveying the **meaning** "more than one." And learners can indeed make that form-meaning connection from comprehensible input: no "-s" when you talk about one, but you add it to talk about more than one. Is it as easy and simple as it sounds? We wish! If it were, then second language acquisition would be fast, efficient, and universal, when it's actually the opposite. As we will see in the next section, learners rely on just about anything else other than those pesky grammar forms to extract meaning, but there are ways in which we can push them to process things like the plural "-s."

In case you're wondering . . .

Don't we need to teach vocab and grammar differently? If your goal is to help your students develop communicative ability in the target language, then approaching language in such a compartmentalized way won't help. That is precisely why in this book we do not have a chapter on "teaching vocabulary" and a separate one on "teaching grammar." The artificial ways in which textbooks present language have little or nothing to do with second language acquisition, or communication for that matter. When we communicate, we don't preselect structures, and we don't force ourselves to use specific words. Have you ever tried to tell someone what you did last weekend using only "regular" verbs? To interpret and express meaning (i.e., to communicate), we need both vocab and grammar. And we indeed acquire both through form-meaning connections.

Focus on Form

We know that learners use input to make form-meaning connections, and that applies to both vocab and grammar. However, some forms come up less frequently in the input than others. So how can learners get grammar from the input when it comes to those rare specimens? Also, input only tells them what's possible in the target language, but not what's *not* possible. For example, in English, you can say "pick me up" but not "pick up me." Can learners figure that out from the input alone, especially if it's different from another language they speak? Enter focus on form. Wait . . . grammar teaching? Not in the traditional sense. Keep reading.

Form-focused instruction is an umbrella term to refer to "any pedagogical effort to draw learners' attention to language either implicitly or explicitly" (Spada, 1997, p. 73). Not all form-focused instruction is created equal. Long (1991) distinguished two main categories of form-focused instruction:

- **Focus on Forms (FonFs):** Within FonFs, the language is the object to be studied, the forms are preselected (e.g., "today we'll learn direct object pronouns"), and grammar is taught explicitly and intentionally.
- **Focus on Form (FonF):** Within FonF, the language is viewed as a tool to express meaning, and attention to grammar happens while communicating.

The consensus is that FonF is better than FonFs. However, this consensus has not been easy to reach, and some people still defend FonFs. There's been a lot of research on this topic and just about as much—or more—debate among language educators. It's easy to get overwhelmed when the experts can't seem to agree, but we'll simplify things and go point by point.

First, explicit instruction is **not necessary** for acquisition. There is zero evidence indicating that without explicit grammar instruction, people cannot acquire a language. Of course, they can!

The question is: is it *helpful*? Perhaps the better question would be: helpful for what? Studies claiming that explicit grammar instruction is helpful for language learning tend to measure "language learning" as the correct application of a rule students just learned in very explicit conditions (i.e., not while engaged in communication, as defined in Chapter 1). In other words, explicit grammar instruction might be helpful for students to do well on exams that require them to conjugate verbs correctly.

But let's not lose sight of our goal: acquisition. At the core of this debate, is the question of whether explicit knowledge (i.e., knowledge of the rules) influences the development of implicit knowledge (i.e., acquisition). Some scholars believe that being taught the rules and "practicing" contributes to language development (DeKeyser, 2014). However, this position is based on the assumption that language acquisition is the same as learning anything else, and most SLA scholars do not agree with that assumption. Other experts claim that explicit knowledge might be helpful when it comes to structures that were partially acquired (implicitly!) before receiving explicit instruction, but not for "new" structures (Ellis & Shintani, 2014). This view is basically another way of saying that the bulk of language acquisition happens implicitly and not as a result of explicit instruction. Does this mean explicit grammar instruction might be helpful for more advanced learners? The jury is still out on that one.

Can we at least settle the grammar-teaching debate for novice and intermediate learners? Here's what we would like you to take away from this section:

- There is no *need* for explicit grammar instruction in the traditional sense (presentation-practice-production) if our goal is to help students acquire the language.

- Research is biased toward measuring explicit knowledge, and taking results out of context is a sure-fire way of reaching misleading conclusions. If your objectives do not include students claiming they can recite grammar rules or verb paradigms, then be careful with any research-based claims about explicit instruction being beneficial.

- Teaching learners the rules does not speed up the acquisition process. If explicit grammar instruction takes time away from engaging in meaningful communication (i.e., understanding or conveying meaning), then we might actually be slowing things down.

- Give priority to understanding content over understanding rules. Plan your lessons around communicative goals, rather than a list of grammar structures to cover.

- Drawing the learners' attention to grammatical forms within the course of meaningful communication might facilitate language development because it might help learners make or strengthen the appropriate form-meaning connections. Why do we keep saying "might" and not "will"? Because, as we saw in Chapter 1, nothing guarantees acquisition.

> **In case you're wondering . . .**
>
> Is it better to have students discover the rule themselves? Although an induc-
> tive approach (i.e., drawing the learners' attention to patterns in the input and
> guiding them to formulate possible explanations for what they notice) may
> seem appealing because it is learner centered, it is still a form of explicit gram-
> mar instruction, where the language is the object of discussion. If your goal is
> for learners to be able to state rules, then it is probably better to spend more
> class time co-constructing the rules as opposed to telling students what the
> rules are. But if your goal is for students to develop communicative ability in
> the target language, then discussing rules and language patterns might not
> be the best use of class time. Knowing a rule doesn't mean you can use it, and
> there is no correlation between the ability to formulate grammar explanations
> and language proficiency.

One last thing before we conclude the grammar-teaching debate: Some students might tell you that they *want* to know the rules. Most likely, that's because
it's what they have come to expect in a language class, rather than any actual
cognitive benefits. Some learners also want the teacher to translate everything
for them, but we know that won't help them acquire the language. Therefore, we
need to be careful about making pedagogical decisions based solely on learners'
beliefs or preferences.

That being said, we are not advocating to ignore students if they ask you something related to grammar. In fact, the vast majority of SLA experts would agree
that "focus on form can at least be beneficial to most if not all learners if it is
informed by what we know about processes involved in acquisition" (Wong &
VanPatten, 2003, p. 418). The issue arises when form dictates your curriculum
and lesson content.

All we are saying is: Give communication a chance. Lead with meaningful
content and comprehensible input that students are compelled to understand,
and, if, in the course of communicating, the need arises to clarify something
grammar related (e.g., "the plural of goose is geese"), go for it.

Structured Input Activities

Processing the input for meaning is fundamental, but our students can only process so much information at a time. How can we help them make the most out
of the input, especially when it comes to getting "grammar" from it? This is where
knowing about Processing Instruction (VanPatten, 1996) is very useful. This

approach is based on a series of principles and sub-principles that outline how learners process input. Here are two of the principles that will prove the most useful as you create input activities:

- Learners process the input for meaning first and foremost. They will first process content words (vocab, if you will), and if that's good enough, then they might not even notice anything else.
  - For example: If I say, "I have four dogs," you understand there is more than one without even noticing the little "-s" attached to the word "dog." And it's not because you have superpowers; it's because I gave you that information elsewhere in the sentence ("four"). However, if I said, "I love my dogs," you would have to process that little "-s" to understand that I have more than one dog.
  - Other examples: "Last night" gives away the meaning of "pastness," "tomorrow" gives away the meaning of "future," etc.

- Learners are more likely to process a form that appears first, as opposed to in the middle of an utterance. In other words, they're less likely to skip the first thing they see or hear, and that can help make forms more salient in the input.
  - For example: Contrast these two ways of playing Two Truths and a Lie (where learners must guess which statement is false). In which of the two options do you see "used to be" in a more salient way?

Option A	Option B
Prof. Henshaw used to be a line-dance instructor. Prof. Henshaw used to be a high school teacher. Prof. Henshaw used to be a dog trainer.	Prof. Henshaw . . . . . . used to be a line-dance instructor. . . . used to be a high school teacher. . . . used to be a dog trainer.

In Option A, the phrase "used to be" gets buried in the middle of the sentence. Meanwhile, in option B, you're less likely to skip over it since it's the first thing you read. (P.S. The false statement is the second one.)

If you are not fully convinced, try this with your students: Tell them a very simple story (four to five sentences) twice. Then, ask them to write the story verbatim, relying on memory only. What's the part most of them got right? Chances are it's the very beginning and the very end.

Keeping these two principles in mind, we can create activities that present the input in a way that it is "manipulated to push learners to process something they might miss otherwise" (VanPatten, 2017, p. 106). Those types of activities are called "structured input" activities, which follow a set of guidelines that will make a lot of sense for any type of input activity you create. Plus, research has shown that structured input can indeed help learners make the right form-meaning connections, and who doesn't want that?

Here we will paraphrase and summarize the guidelines to create structured input activities:

- **Don't overwhelm them.**
  - Focus on only one form (e.g., first-person singular, present tense) or one contrast (e.g., third-person singular and plural) per activity. Careful: This doesn't correspond to the artificial division of language in textbooks. So, for instance, it's OK to include regular and irregular verbs.
  - Keep statements short and simple.

- **Don't forget about meaning.**
  - Avoid random sentences without any purpose other than to practice grammar.
  - Provide a cohesive and meaningful context for the items within each activity.

- **Keep in mind how learners process input.**
  - Put the form at the beginning of the utterance.
  - Don't include content words or context clues that will give away whatever the form conveys. Force learners to process the form as much as possible.

- **Include written (reading) and aural (listening) input.**
  - Typically, moving from written to aural input is best, although it depends on the language.
  - It's OK if one activity contains only written input and another only aural input. But we should remember to include both types.

And, of course, learners should be **able and compelled** to understand the input. The teacher should have a way to verify that they're understanding and processing the form correctly. The two examples below will help you understand exactly what we mean.

In the first example, learners must interpret the verbs correctly to answer, which helps them make the right form-meaning connections.

Dogs, just like people, have a daily routine. But not all dogs have the same routine, even if they live together. Max, a black lab, lives with two other dogs: Charlie and Emma.

Step 1: Which of these statements describe something only Max does, and which ones describe something all three dogs do every day?

Only Max	All three dogs	
☐	☐	. . . wakes up at 6:00 a.m.
☐	☐	. . . go for a walk
☐	☐	. . . eats breakfast
☐	☐	. . . plays in the yard
☐	☐	. . . goes to the dog park
☐	☐	. . . take medicine
☐	☐	. . . eat dinner at 5:00
☐	☐	. . . go to bed at 9:00
☐	☐	. . . sleeps on the couch

Step 2: Based on what you now know about Max's routine, would you say he is a couch potato or a high-energy dog?

Let's pause for a minute to clarify a few things about the example above:

- Did you notice that we didn't include each verb twice (once singular, once plural)? It's not a necessary condition for structured input. It doesn't mean we couldn't do that, but as long as some actions are in third-person singular and others in third-person plural, that's enough to help learners notice the contrast between the two.

- Did you notice that some verbs appear more than once? That's perfectly OK. Instead of focusing on how many different verbs or exceptions you've included, think about meaning first and foremost. We use the verb "to go" to convey lots of things, so it is natural for that verb to appear multiple times.

- Did you notice that students must process the form ("take," "plays") to interpret the statements correctly, and they can't rely on what's more likely based on context? We're being extra sneaky by including some actions that you might expect all three dogs to do, but they're in third-person singular. If, for instance, students selected "All three dogs" for the item "plays in the yard," then you would know they're not processing the verb ending ("-s"), or perhaps they think this "-s" means plural. By drawing their attention to it and pushing them to process it, you are increasing the likelihood that they will make that particular form-meaning connection. Does it guarantee that they will now conjugate all verbs correctly? Nothing can guarantee that.

- Did you notice that students are just telling you if it's something only Max does or all three dogs do, rather than whether the verbs are "third-person singular" or "third-person plural"? That's because we want students to make the right form-meaning connections, not the form-form connections. When we communicate, we express meaning even if we are completely unaware of terminology like "third-person singular," "dative case," or "present-perfect continuous." So, in structured input activities, what the students do with the input should be **meaning-based**, and not about grammatical terminology.

- Did you notice that we didn't have a gazillion items? Even though no guideline says how many items should be in each activity, between 8 and 15 is probably a good rule of thumb. Having more than 15 items tends to make the activity tedious. It's better to have learners do several structured input activities rather than only one activity with too many items.

In this second example, even though learners will likely process the whole thing for meaning only (content words), they are exposed to the form we want them to focus on in a meaningful context, helping to strengthen the form-meaning connections they initially made with activities like the one in the first example above.

Step 1: How well do you know your instructor's country? Complete the statements based on what you know, or think.

Argentina . . .

. . . is located near_____.

. . . is bigger than _____.

. . . is smaller than _____.

. . . is famous for _____.

. . . has _____ million people.

Step 2: Your instructor will now confirm your answers. Based on the number of responses you got right, how well do you know your instructor's country?

One thing you may have noticed is that, in the second example, the students are writing something, but it's not output because they are not producing the form we are secretly targeting. Even in Step 2, they don't have to spontaneously produce the form.

It's important to clarify that students would not be ready to start interacting or producing the forms after only two activities like these. Novice learners in particular will need to spend a lot more class time on input before they are ready for output. In fact, these two examples are only providing sentence-level written input, which is clearly not enough. Within the context of a lesson or unit, you should include aural input and move from sentences to connected discourse.

In a nutshell

Before we move on to classroom examples, summarize five main points from this chapter. What are your own takeaways?

_____

_____

_____

_____

Would you like to learn more?
Go to **www.hackettpublishing.com/common-ground-resources**
for a list of suggested readings, webinars, and other resources.

What Does It Look Like in the Classroom?

Example 1: Day 1 of Class

This example serves to demonstrate how the teacher can make input comprehensible with novice learners from day 1, without resorting to frequent translations. Some things to notice in this example are: the use of gestures and visuals, the repetition of key phrases, the simplification of statements and questions, and the fact that students are involved and held accountable for paying attention to the meaning of the utterances, without asking them to produce anything but proper names or choices given by the teacher. Depending on the language you teach, you might also be able to use cognates to help students understand as well. In the case of college courses, the part about "favorite subjects" could be modified to be about the students' majors or minors.

Proficiency level: Novice-low

Teacher: Hi! (*waves hello*) How are you? (*shows a scale with a happy face on one extreme and an unhappy face on the other, with the phrases "very well," "so-so," "not good" along the scale*). I am (*points to herself*) very well! (*points to the happy face, makes a thumbs-up gesture, and smiles*). How are you? (*emphasis on "you," points to the students*) Are you (*emphasis on "you"*) very well (*points to the happy face, and makes a thumbs-up gesture*), "so-so" (*points to the middle of the scale, and makes a gesture with her hand*), or "not good" (*points to the unhappy face, makes a thumbs-down gesture, and frowns*)? How are you? (*points to the students*) Very well (*points to the happy face on the scale and smiles*), yes? (*makes a thumbs-up gesture*)

Students: Very well, yes.

Teacher: Excellent! (*gives them two thumbs-up and smiles*) My name (*points to herself*) is Laura Smith. (*writes down "Laura Smith" on the board*) My name is Laura. (*looks at a student*) Is your (*emphasis on "your," points to the student*) name Laura? Yes (*nods*) or no (*shakes head*)? Your (*emphasis on "your" and points*) name . . . Is your name Laura?

Student: No.

Teacher: Ah! What is your (*emphasis on "your" and points*) name? My (*points to herself*) name is Laura. What is your (*emphasis on "your" and points*) name?

Student: Jessica.

Teacher: Hi Jessica! Nice to meet you (*shakes student's hand*).

Student: Yes . . .?

Teacher (*to the whole class*): Her name is Jessica (*points to the student*). My name is Laura (*points to herself; writes the phrase "My name is Laura" on the board; looks at another student*). What is your name? (*emphasis on "your" and points*)

Student: Your name . . . Michael.

Teacher: Hi Michael! Nice to meet you (*shakes student's hand*). Michael, how are you? Very well, so-so, or not good? (*points to the scale*)

Michael: So-so.

Teacher: Oh no! (*makes a sad face*)

The class continues in this way, as the teacher greets a few other students.

Teacher (*to the whole class*): What is her (*points to a student*) name? Her name. What is her name?

Students: Jessica!

Teacher: Ah, yes! Her name is Jessica! And his name? (*points to a student*)

Students: Michael!

Teacher: Ah, yes, yes! Michael! And what is my name? (*points to herself*)

Students: Laura!

Teacher: Yes, my name is Laura. I love (*draws a heart on the board*) languages: English, Spanish, French, Korean, Arabic—All languages! Jessica, do you like (*points to the heart*) languages too? Yes? (*makes a thumbs-up gesture*) Or no? (*makes a thumbs-down gesture*)

Jessica: Yes.

Teacher: Excellent! And you, Michael, do you like languages, too?

Michael: No . . .

Teacher: Oh, I see. So, your favorite subject is not languages. (*writes "favorite subject" and the translation on the board*) Your favorite subject is not (*emphasis on "not"*) languages. What is your favorite subject? Math? (*shows a picture with equations and a calculator*) Do you like (*makes a thumbs-up gesture*) math? (*points to the picture*)

Michael: No!

Teacher: Oh! What is your favorite subject? (*shows a list of subjects in the target language, with their corresponding translations or accompanied by a picture, if they are cognates*)

Michael: History.

Teacher: Very good! I like (*makes a thumbs-up gesture*) history, too! But my favorite subject is languages. (*writes "My favorite subject is . . ." on the board*)

I love (*points to the heart*) languages. (*looks at another student*) Alicia, what is your favorite subject? (*writes "What is your favorite subject?" on the board, directly above "My favorite subject is . . ."*) What is your favorite subject? (*emphasis on "your," then points to the list of subjects*)

Alicia: Math.

Teacher: Excellent!

The class continues in this way; the teacher asks a few more students about their names and favorite subjects. Then, the teacher gives students a chart where they have to list the names and favorite subjects of five of their classmates. The teacher first models what to write in each column with the information of one of the students in the class.

Example 2: Introducing a New Topic

This example serves to demonstrate how the teacher can make input comprehensible with novice learners when introducing a new topic or unit, staying as much as possible in the target language. In this example, the teacher uses mainly gestures and visuals, including writing things down. You will also notice a lot of repetition and rephrasing. Depending on the language you teach, you might also be able to use cognates to help students understand. When introducing a new topic, it is best to keep the information load as low as possible. Even if students had previously learned about breakfast foods, for instance, it's better not to reference them at this point; later in the lesson, however, it would be a great idea to reference them for a more extended treatment of the topic and "recycling" what students know. One important thing to notice in this example is how the teacher actively involves the students throughout the introduction of the topic, as opposed to providing one big lecture followed by questions. The teacher's binary-choice questions keep students focused on meaning while checking for comprehension in an adequate way for the students' level.

Proficiency level: Novice-high

The teacher shows a blank schedule like the one below.

    6:00 _____
    6:30 _____
    7:00 _____
    7:30 _____
    (more times listed)

Teacher: Today we are going to talk about our daily routines. This is my schedule. (*points to the clock, then to himself*) Do you think my schedule is busy or easy? Is it busy, too many things to do? Or is it easy, with a lot of free time?

Students: Busy!

Teacher: Yes, it is busy. It is not very easy. I wake up (*stretches his arms, mimicking waking up*) early. Do you think I wake up at 6 a.m. or 9 a.m.?

Students: 6 a.m.

Teacher: Yes, yes; I wake up at 6 a.m. (*writes "wake up" on the schedule, next to 6:00*) I wake up early because I have to be at school early. What time do teachers have to be at school? At 7:30 or 8:30?

Students: 7:30.

Teacher: Yes! So, I wake up at 6:30 (*points to the schedule*), and I take the bus (*shows a picture of a bus*) at 7:00 (*writes on the schedule*). I have to be at school by 7:30 a.m. (*writes on the schedule*) But before I go, I need caffeine. I LOVE coffee (*holds up a coffee mug*). I drink a lot of coffee. How many cups do you think I drink? One, two, or three cups?

Students: Two cups?

Teacher: No—I really love coffee! I drink three cups! But I don't like to eat a big breakfast (*shows a picture of a breakfast*). I don't like (*makes a thumbs-down gesture*) a big breakfast. I eat a small (*makes a hand gesture indicating "small"*) breakfast. How many students here eat a small breakfast, too? Raise your hand (*teacher raises his hand to model*). Who eats a small breakfast?

Some students raise their hands, and the teacher counts.

Teacher: Not very many! Only five students eat a small breakfast. I don't eat a big breakfast because I don't have time (*points to his watch and makes a gesture indicating no*). I wake up at 6:30 (*points to the schedule*), and I take the bus at 7:00 (*points to the schedule*).

The teacher introduces more of his schedule, writing keywords, as needed, and asking simple questions to keep the learners engaged.

At the end, students indicate if a series of statements are true or false, presented as structured input.

Mr. Henkins . . .

> . . . sleeps eight hours each night.
> . . . eats a big breakfast.
> . . . drinks a lot of coffee.
> (more statements like that)

The lesson continues with additional interpretive communication activities, as described in Example 1 of Chapter 2.

Example 3: Engaging Students with Authentic Resources

This example illustrates the use of an authentic resource, in this case, a menu, as a source of input. This activity is not the introduction to the unit, but rather one more way to continue providing input after students have had a chance to learn words related to food and drinks. It's not necessary for the students to understand all of the menu, but the teacher should make sure that most of the items are either familiar to the students or made comprehensible through visuals. In preparation for this activity, the teacher selects a restaurant menu in the target language and prints out a few copies. Then, the menu should be cut up into several sections, each one containing just one dish and its description, so that students can work together in small groups to reconstruct the original menu. A similar activity could be done with schedules (movies, trains, etc.), supermarket flyers, classified ads, etc.

Proficiency level: Novice-high/intermediate-low

Teacher: Today, we are going to look at a menu from a restaurant in [*country*]. But first, you need to help me. This menu is in pieces. (*shows students the strips of paper*) Every dish is on a separate piece of paper. It's very hard to read it this way. Help me put it back together. First, decide if the dish is an appetizer, an entrée, or a dessert. For example (*shows students one of the strips of paper and reads it*), chocolate cake with fresh berries . . . is that an appetizer, entrée, or dessert?

Student: Dessert!

Teacher: Right! OK, let's put it in the dessert section. Now (*grabs another strip of paper and reads it*), linguine with shrimp and vegetables. Do we put it with desserts, too?

Students: No! Entrée!

Teacher: Very good! OK, work with a classmate to finish categorizing all of these other dishes.

The teacher distributes the rest of the strips of paper to the groups and circulates around the room making sure that students are putting the dishes in the correct category. After students have classified the items successfully, the teacher gets the students' attention to continue with the activity.

Teacher: Now that we have them in the right category, we need to put them in order, from the cheapest to the most expensive. For example, we have three desserts: chocolate cake with fresh berries, an ice cream sundae, and a fruit salad. What do you think? What is probably (*emphasis on "probably"*) the cheapest: cake, ice cream, or fruit salad?

Students: Fruit salad!

Teacher: Yes, I agree. So, we put fruit salad first. And then? What goes next? Is the chocolate cake cheaper or more expensive than the ice cream sundae?

Students: More expensive!

Teacher: Yes, it's probably more expensive. So, we need to put the desserts in this order (*writes on the board*): fruit salad, ice cream sundae, and chocolate cake. They are in order from cheapest to most expensive. From the lowest price (*writes "$" next to "fruit salad"*) to the highest price (*writes "$$$" next to "chocolate cake"*). OK, your turn! (*points to the students*) Put the dishes of each category in order, from the cheapest to the most expensive.

Students rank the dishes within each category. When they have finished, the teacher reveals the actual prices from the original menu to verify whether students had them in the correct order. To conclude the activity, the teacher asks students to determine if the restaurant would be good for someone who is a vegetarian, someone on a budget, someone with kids, etc.

Example 4: Working with Infographics

This example serves to demonstrate how the teacher can engage students in understanding an infographic that includes icons, percentages, and short phrases (e.g., "play video games"). To have the students do something with the information, the teacher covered or removed some of the icons and percentages so students could guess, match, or draw the numbers and icons that correspond with each phrase. At the beginning of the activity, the teacher asks a few comprehension questions (mainly binary-choice questions) based on the information students can see, just so the students are able to get a sense of the content of the infographic before moving on to guessing the missing percentages and drawing the missing icons. Please note: The percentages mentioned here are for illustrative purposes only.

Proficiency level: Novice-high/intermediate-low

The teacher shows students an infographic showing what teenagers from a country where the target language is spoken do in their free time, on average, with percentages and icons. However, four of the icons are missing, and four of the numbers representing the percentages are also blank. Other icons and percentages are intact.

Teacher: This is how teenagers in [*country*] spend their free time. These are their pastimes. For example, 48% of them play video games (*points to the corresponding place on the infographic showing the percentage, icon, and phrase "play video games").* Is that a lot or a little?

Students: A lot!

Teacher: Yes, I agree. Now, let's look at reading (*points to the corresponding place on the infographic*). Do more of them play video games or read? (*points back and forth to the two percentages on the infographic*)

Students: Video games!

Teacher: That's right. 48% of them play video games (*point to the right place on the infographic*) and only 24% read in their free time. Do you think that's similar to the United States? Is it the same here in the U.S.? (*writes the "equal" sign on the board*) Probably similar or probably different?

Students: Similar!

Teacher: I agree. It is probably similar, right? And what about working out? (*points to an icon that corresponds with "working out," but there is no percentage next to it*) There's no number! What do you think? (*writes four percentages on the board: 13%, 5%, 20%, 2%*). Which number goes with each activity? (*points to the percentages on the board, and then the blank spaces on the infographic*) What number probably (*emphasis on "probably"*) corresponds with "working out"? What do you think: 13%, 5%, 20%, or 2%?

Some students say: 13%!

Other students say: 2%!

Teacher: Raise your hand if you say "13%" (*teacher counts*). Raise your hand if you say 2% (*teacher counts*). The majority says 13%, and that's right! Thirteen percent of them work out. (*checks off 13% on the board*) Now, what about bike riding? How many of them like to ride their bikes in their free time? (*points to the remaining percentages on the board, and then the icon that corresponds with "bike riding" on the infographic*)

The lesson continues as students guess the other percentages.

Teacher: Now, there are other activities (*points to the blanks that represent missing icons*), but they don't have icons. It's incomplete. We need icons! You (*points to the students*) are going to draw (*makes a gesture*) icons for these activities: watching TV, going out to eat, sleeping, dancing.

The teacher provides further input by showing the percentages for similar activities in another country and asks students to compare the two, either with true/false or multiple-choice questions. The teacher could also do a structured input activity, where students rank the activities according to the frequency with which they do them, similar to Example 2 in Chapter 1.

Example 5: Input Bracketing

This example serves to demonstrate input bracketing, which is similar to what is done during sports tournaments (e.g., March Madness, World Cup). But, instead of teams, the choices are words in the target language, such as foods, activities, places, clothing, etc. The "winners" are determined based on students' preferences. The activity begins with an empty bracket, and the teacher writes each competing pair of options as she mentions them. Students vote by raising their hand or standing up, a simple majority wins, and the teacher writes the winner in the winner space. The goal is to choose one overall winner. The way brackets work implies repeated exposure to the same vocab items or structures (e.g., who prefers), which is great for language acquisition. If needed, the teacher could include pictures along with the choices to help students understand.

Proficiency level: Novice-mid

Teacher: Today, we are going to plan a party (*shows a picture of a birthday party*). First, the food! (*shows them a picture of various foods*) Mmmmm! So many choices! What food do you prefer? You (*points to the students*) are going to vote. Raise your hand (*raises her hand to show them what to do*) to vote for your favorite. OK? First, hamburgers or hot dogs. Who prefers hamburgers? Raise your hand (*raises her hand to show them what to do*) if you prefer hamburgers.

Students raise their hands, and the teacher counts and writes the number on the board.

Teacher: 10 people prefer hamburgers. Now, who prefers hot dogs? Stand up (*gestures with her hands indicating an upward motion*) if you prefer hot dogs.

Students stand up. The teacher counts and writes the number on the board.

Teacher: 8 people prefer hot dogs. Hamburgers win! (*writes hamburgers in the first winner spot*) Now, tacos or burritos? Raise your hand if you prefer tacos.

Students raise their hands. The teacher counts and writes the number on the board.

Teacher: 12 people prefer tacos. Now, who prefers burritos? Stand up (*gestures with her hands indicating an upward motion*).

Students stand up. The teacher counts and writes the number on the board.

Teacher: 6 people prefer burritos. Tacos win! (*writes "tacos" in the second winner spot*) Now, pizza or chicken wings?

Students continue to vote for their favorite, one pair at a time, until the bracket is complete, like this one:

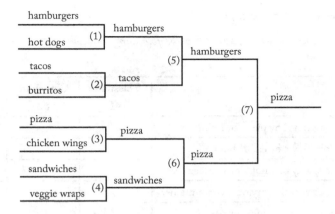

Teacher: We are going to have pizza at the party! Excellent! I love pizza! Thanks for helping me decide. Now, we need to choose an activity for the party (*shows a picture of various games and activities that take place at parties*). So many choices! Let's vote again. First, what do you prefer: to play charades or to play *Pictionary?*

A new bracket is created, which can be bigger or smaller, depending on the number of choices given at the beginning. The final choice is selected using the same procedure as above. Other brackets can be done for when to have the party, what music to listen to, etc. After all choices have been made, students use the information to create invitations to the party. The teacher should provide sentence starters to scaffold output.

Example 6: Class Surveys

This example illustrates a way to do class surveys conducted by the students themselves; however, it is still an input activity because the teacher prepares the questions, and the students only need to read them aloud; the students being interviewed answer by stating their choice (i.e., they are not creating with language). In this example, students indicate their travel preferences by answering binary-choice questions. At higher proficiency levels, students could indicate their level or agreement or disagreement with a series of statements, the frequency with which they do or did certain activities, or even provide names (brands, places, celebrities) as the answers to the questions. Also, in this example, all the students see all the questions, but another alternative would be to have each student in charge of "researching" a different topic or question; this way, everyone gets asked something new. In that case, each student would ask 10 classmates, collect their responses, and then report their findings by calculating the percentage of classmates who chose each option.

Proficiency level: Novice-high

The students each receive a paper with the following questions written in the target language:

	Classmate #1	Classmate #2	Classmate #3
Do you prefer to travel by plane or train?			
Do you prefer to travel by car or bus?			
Do you prefer to stay in a hotel or with family?			
Do you prefer to visit the city or the mountains?			
Do you prefer to visit museums or parks?			
Do you prefer a window seat or an aisle seat?			

Teacher: Today, we are going to talk about our travel preferences. You are going to interview three classmates. As you interview each person, write down their answer here (*shows students the grid with questions and answers, pointing to the empty slots*). For example (*teacher looks at one student*): Sophie, do you prefer to travel by plane or train?

Sophie: Plane.

Teacher: Plane! Got it! (*pretends to write on the paper she is holding*) Now (*looks at another student*), Robert, do you prefer to travel by plane or train?

Robert: Plane.

Teacher: Plane! Again! (*pretends to write on the paper she is holding*) OK, your turn! For each question, ask three people and write their answers.

Students proceed to ask each other the questions and record the answers that their partners give them. The teacher circulates to make sure students are on task and to help them, if needed. When students have completed the grid, they return to their seats.

Teacher: Very good! Now I want to know your results. What trends did you find? Complete the following sentences based on your results (*displays the following sentence starters so students can report their findings*). Tell me only three trends:

None of my classmates prefer _____.

Most of my classmates prefer _____.

All of my classmates prefer _____.

As students share their results, the teacher could see if other groups found the same or not, and try to uncover the preferences of the entire class.

Example 7: Storytelling with Drawing

This example shows a nonverbal way for the teacher to check for understanding. As the teacher tells a very simple story, students are drawing what she is saying. Given that drawing what someone is saying takes time, the teacher should tell the story slowly and repeat key phrases frequently. Even though students don't have to show that they're understanding every single word, their drawings have to make sense for the plot of the story. A typical story pattern involves the introduction and description of a main character, the problem they have, the things they try to solve it, and the final outcome (i.e., the problem was solved or not). The complexity of the story can be modified to match the students' proficiency level.

Proficiency level: Novice-high

Teacher: Today, I will tell you a story about a boy named George. You (*points to the students*) will listen (*does a gesture pointing to her ear*), and you will draw it (*demonstrates drawing on the board*). You need paper (*holds up a piece of paper*) and pencil (*holds up a pencil*). Your drawings can be simple, but show you understand. Let's do the first part together. There is a boy named George. (*draws a boy on the board*) OK? You draw! There is a boy named George. (*pauses and waits for students to get started if some of them are not understanding*) George has a problem. George has a big problem (*emphasis on "big"*). George doesn't have shoes! (*points to her own shoes*) George doesn't have shoes.

As the teacher is telling the story, she walks around and checks the drawings, making sure they match the story but also praising students. As she is circulating throughout the classroom, she notices that one student drew a boy with shoes on.

Teacher: Sarah, careful. George doesn't (*emphasis on "doesn't"*) have shoes (*points to the shoes on the student's drawing*).

Student: Oh! (*student corrects her drawing*)

Teacher: Very good. George doesn't have shoes. George goes to a store. George goes to Gracy's (*pauses and waits for students to draw*) George goes to Gracy's.

The teacher walks around and checks the drawings. If any of the students didn't include "Gracy's" on their drawings, the teacher asks them to include the name of the store since it's important for the rest of the story.

Teacher: But there is another (*emphasis on "another"*) problem! Gracy's only has very, very, very small shoes. Too small for George! Gracy's only has very small shoes.

The teacher walks around and checks the drawings, making sure students included the details that are important for the rest of the story.

Teacher: So . . . George goes to another store (*pauses and waits for students to draw*). George goes to Nord's. But there is a problem again! Nord's only has very, very, very big shoes. Huge shoes! (*does a gesture accompanying the word "huge"*) Nord's only has very big shoes. Too big for George!

The teacher walks around and checks the drawings.

Teacher: Poor George! George is sad. (*makes a sad face and points to the students' drawings to signal that they should include that detail*) George is very sad. George goes home. George goes home without shoes. (*pauses and waits for students to draw*) George looks online. George looks on Zapatos.com. (*pauses and waits for students to draw*) Zapatos has shoes! Zapatos has lots of shoes. Perfect for George! George buys shoes on Zapatos.com. And now George has shoes!

The teacher walks around and checks the drawings. Once everyone has finished, the teacher asks students to vote for the best title for the story, out of three options, which she writes on the board or displays for students to see. Option A: "Shoeless George"; option B: "Shoes for George"; option C: "Shopping with George."

Example 8: Logic Puzzles

Logic puzzles are a fun way to engage learners in understanding the target language. They can be as simple or as complex as needed to match the proficiency level of the students, and they can also be written in a way that they focus on one particular structure (e.g., past tense, comparisons) and topic (e.g., food, pastimes, travel, family, etc.). Each student needs to deduce the relationships between different people, places, or things based on the oral or written clues the teacher provides. Students fill in the grid with Xs and Os to determine the solution. Students could work individually or in teams, and the whole class could be turned into a relay race: As teams finish one logic puzzle, they show it to their teacher, and if it's correct, then they are given a new one to solve. The team that solves the most puzzles within a specific time limit wins!

Proficiency level: Novice-high/intermediate-low

		Age			Birthday		
		16	17	20	January	July	October
Name	Mary						
	Sam						
	Joe						
Birthday	January						
	July						
	October						

- Sam is not the oldest.
- This person's birthday is on a month that starts with the same letter as his name.
- The oldest person's birthday is in winter.
- Joe is younger than Sam.

Example 9: Memory Games

This example is one variation of a "memory game," where students are asked to look at an image for a couple of minutes and try to remember as many details as possible. Then, the teacher hides the images and tests the students' visual memory through a series of questions that follow the guidelines of structured input: The forms of the present progressive are the first thing that students see in each line. In preparation for this activity, the teacher should find an image (a painting, photograph, drawing, map, etc.) with several elements and details. It can be an authentic resource, but not necessarily. In this example, the teacher is using the present progressive; however, the complexity and focus of the input can be modified to fit the proficiency level of the students. Also, their visual memory can be tested in a variety of ways, depending on the image. For example, if it is a drawing of multiple people doing various activities, with their names displayed next to each one, the teacher could ask students to match the name of the person with the activity they were doing in the image.

Proficiency level: Novice-high

Teacher: Today, we will look at a painting called *La Feria en Reynosa*. This artist is Carmen Lomas Garza. (*displays the painting*) What do you think? Do you like it?

Students: Yes!

Teacher: It's very colorful. How many people do you see in this painting? How many people in total?

Some students: 18!

Other students: No, 17!

Other students: No, 19!

Teacher: A lot of people! Look at the painting carefully. There are a lot of small details, a lot of things going on in this painting. OK, so let's see who is good at spotting details. Who has a good visual memory? Let's see. Look at the painting for two minutes. Don't write anything! Just look at it and try to memorize it.

Students look at the painting in silence. After two minutes, the teacher turns off the projector, and gives students a handout with questions that each student answers individually.

Teacher: Let's see who has good visual memory. Write down your answers. Careful! Sometimes, the answer can be zero!

How many people . . .

> . . . are eating?
>
> . . . are cooking food?
>
> . . . are playing an instrument?
>
> . . . are wearing a hat?
>
> . . . are playing with a dog?

After all students write down their answers, the teacher displays the painting again and helps students verify the correct answers for each question. To conclude, the teacher determines who has good visual memory based on the number of correct answers.

Now That You Know

Discussion and Expansion Questions

1) At the beginning of the chapter, we provided several examples of what counts and doesn't count as input for acquisition. Now, let's try this activity: For three minutes straight, brainstorm more examples for either of the two columns. Write examples down in the appropriate category (counts or doesn't count) as you think of them. After the three minutes have passed, review the examples you wrote. Was it easier to think of examples of input that counts or doesn't count? Why do you think that is?

2) Below are three common reasons why teachers inadvertently provide input that is too hard for students to understand. Which of these reasons resonates the most with you, in your experience as either a learner or a teacher?

   a) Going too fast: Teachers assume that after a couple of input activities, learners are ready to move on to something new.

   b) Forgetting what it's like to be at their level: It's hard for language educators, who are at an advanced/superior proficiency level, to realize that even the simplest of sentences could be incomprehensible to a novice-level learner.

   c) Not having realistic proficiency goals: Some teachers have realistic expectations when it comes to oral production, but they expect much more in terms of interpretive communication (listening or reading).

3) In this chapter, we talked about only one of the five hypotheses that made up Krashen's Monitor Model. What are the other four? And which one do you think has been criticized the most and the least?

4) In this chapter, we discussed different strategies to make the input comprehensible. Would the type of strategy you use vary according to the proficiency level of the students or the language you teach? What other factors could influence the strategies you choose? And thinking of gestures or facial expressions in particular, are there any that your students would understand but might be offensive in the target-language culture?

5) Describe how you could help learners understand the following phrases in the language you teach, without translating:

   a) "Open the book to page 11."

   b) "What you need to do now is put the sentences in order."

    c) "Compare your answers with a classmate."

    d) "Let's see who can remember."

Explain whether you would simplify any of the phrases, rely on cognates, use body language/gestures, or incorporate visuals. Feel free to use more than one strategy!

6) Let's explore a little more the presence of the shared language (other than the target language) in language classrooms, which is tightly connected to the topic of input.

    a) Why do you think some experts don't agree with the practice of using the shared language to make "important announcements," while relegating the target language to "activities"?

    b) Some topics are important for students to know about, but they are well above the students' proficiency level. Educators have a tough choice to make: including those important topics in the shared language at the expense of reducing the amount of class time in which the target language is used, or staying all in the target language at the expense of neglecting to talk about those important topics. What is your take on this dilemma? Does one choice have more pros than cons?

    c) What are the pros and cons of using translation as a way to check for comprehension (i.e., asking students to translate what they heard or read so you can make sure they understood)?

7) In 2010, ACTFL issued a statement on the use of the target language in the classroom, which at one point states that "language educators and their students use the target language as exclusively as possible (90% plus) at all levels of instruction." The statement says much more than that, and we recommend reading it in its entirety. Do you fully agree with it? What could be some aspects of it that might merit further discussion? And what do you think prompted ACTFL to make such a statement?

8) Many teachers continue to use a FonFs approach, and most textbooks are organized around a predetermined list of grammar structures because publishing companies claim that's what teachers want. However, for several decades, experts have been making the point that "the process of learning a language would become impossible if every rule out of the thousands that comprise the grammar of a language had to be first learnt as explicit knowledge" (Ellis, 1997, p. 113). Which of the following would you say is the most prevalent reason for the persistence of explicit grammar instruction in language courses? Can you think of others?

a) It's easier to create grammar worksheets and tests than to create comprehension-based lessons and assessments.

b) Instructors and administrators equate "teaching" with "explaining," and so, "teaching a language" = "explaining how the language works."

c) Teachers claim they benefited from explicit grammar instruction themselves, and so will their students.

9) Some high school teachers worry that if they don't teach grammar explicitly, their students won't do well when they get to college or they will score poorly on exams like the Advanced Placement (AP), STAMP, AAPPL, etc. Is that a valid concern? Search for information online to learn more about one of those exams, or ask colleagues who may have experience administering those exams. If you teach college, how would you respond to a high school teacher who expressed these concerns?

10) Go back to the examples we presented in the section "What does it look like in the classroom?" in Chapter 1. Which of them included structured input?

11) We said that learners try to get meaning out of content words (e.g., "four," "tomorrow," "last night," etc.) over grammatical forms (e.g., plural forms, future tense, past tense, etc.). Can you think of other examples that are specific to the language you teach? And how can we structure the input in a way that learners are more likely to process those forms to interpret sentences correctly?

12) Toward the end of the chapter, we said that novice learners "will need to spend a lot more class time on input before they are ready for output." What do you think are some indications that the learners are ready for output?

13) In a few examples in this chapter, we described what a teacher might do to check for understanding and keep learners focused on meaning through binary-choice questions, among other strategies. However, the teacher in our examples never asked a question like this one: "My favorite subject is languages. What is my favorite subject: languages or math?" What could be a potentially problematic aspect of relying primarily on asking questions like that?

Observation and Application Activities

1) Observe an introductory- or intermediate-level class of the language you teach. Take notes on the following:
   a) Out of all of the questions the teacher asked, how many were display questions (the teacher knows the answer to them)?
   b) Were students able and compelled to understand the input the teacher provided? What strategies did the teacher use to make the language comprehensible to the students?
   c) Did the teacher use any authentic resources? If so, how were they made comprehensible, and what did students do with that information?
   d) Could you tell what the goal of the lesson was, other than practicing a particular vocabulary set or grammar structure?
   e) How often did the teacher use the shared language, and for what functions (e.g., announcements, instructions, humor, building rapport with students, explanations, clarification of meaning, etc.)? Considering the level of the students in that class, do you think the instructor could have used the target language for any of those functions instead?

2) Observe an introductory-level class of a language different from the one you teach and preferably not closely related to any other languages you know. Reflect on the experience of being a "learner." Were you able to understand most of what the teacher was saying? If so, what do you think helped you understand the input? If you felt lost at any point, what do you think the teacher could have done to help you understand?

3) Create a structured input activity that would help learners process a particular form in the language you teach, within one of the thematic units in your courses. For example, when talking about travel experiences, you could help learners process past tense through a structured input activity. Remember the guidelines we discussed in this chapter, and don't forget to create a follow-up step that ties it all together and gives students a reason to understand the meaning of the sentences (and not just process the form).

Chapter 4
Reading, Listening, Viewing

Pre-test

Before reading this chapter, indicate whether the following statements are true or false, based on what you know or believe . . . for now!

- Comprehension involves the construction of a single meaning.
- Understanding every word within a text is not enough to conclude that learners will be able to interpret it adequately.
- Top-down processing strategies are more valuable to novice learners than bottom-up processing strategies.
- Guessing words from context is one of the most effective word-level strategies.
- Pre-reading activities should not only help learners activate prior knowledge, but also anticipate and preview the language they will encounter in the text.

Once you have finished or while you are reading this chapter, verify your answers.

WHAT DO I NEED TO KNOW?

The Importance of Interpretive Proficiency

Many textbooks treat reading and listening/viewing as skills to be addressed in supplementary sections, usually at the end of a chapter. However, interpretive communication should not be a corollary to vocab and grammar. As Sparks (2019) notes, "Programs of study and individual course curricula that continue to be organized around a systematic presentation of grammatical patterns and exceptions may not provide a solid foundation on which strong interpretive proficiency (reading and listening comprehension) can develop" (p. 738). Without interpretive proficiency, there is no proficiency in the target language.

One thing you may have noticed in the previous quote is that "interpretive proficiency" seems to be equated with "reading and listening comprehension." As we briefly discussed in Chapter 1, ACTFL proposed distinguishing "comprehension" from "interpretation" primarily to emphasize that engaging with a text goes beyond literal understanding. While we agree 100% with that last part, the need for two different terms is debatable. Comprehension is always much more than the construction of a single meaning (i.e., everyone understands the same thing). It involves understanding not only the meaning of words and sentences, but also the ability to "interpret meaning in relation to background knowledge, interpret and evaluate texts in line with reader goals and purposes" (Grabe, 2014, p. 8). So, whenever we talk about "comprehension" in this chapter, remember that we are using it as synonymous with "interpretive communication" and not limiting it to simple retrieval of information from a text.

Speaking of texts, we should also clarify that "texts" can be any written, oral, or audiovisual material, and they may be authentic or made/modified for learners. For the purposes of acquisition, the authenticity of a text does not matter. Whether or not engaging with authentic texts is important to your curriculum is another story.

Among the benefits of interpretive reading for language development, the expansion of vocabulary is perhaps the most frequently cited and researched. Of course, students won't learn and remember every new word they encounter in a text. Let's not forget how complex language acquisition is! Some studies have suggested that it might take learners more than 10 encounters of that same word to know what it means, know how to spell it, know in what contexts to use it, etc. (Webb, 2007). It is also important to remember that the benefits of reading are not just about *new* vocabulary. As Horst et al. (1998) summarized it, reading can "enrich their knowledge of the words they already know, increase lexical access speeds, build network linkages between words, and . . . a few words will be acquired" (p. 221).

Interpretive-listening activities have many of the same benefits of interpretive reading, but instead of becoming familiar with spelling conventions, learners can hone their phonological perception skills: identifying word/sentence boundaries, recognizing intonation and stress patterns (i.e., prosody), appreciating pronunciation variants, etc. This so-called ear training can help increase listening comprehension, which could in turn contribute to language development.

Engaging with Oral versus Written Texts

As much overlap as there is in terms of the benefits of reading and listening for acquisition, we must acknowledge some important differences between the two.

First, the fleeting nature of oral texts makes us process language in a faster, less meticulous way, whereas we have more time to engage with written texts: We can read and re-read; we can focus on one word and dissect it for as long as we want. When we get tripped up by an unknown word within a written text, we can take time to figure it out and then continue when we're ready. Although it is possible to "pause" some oral texts (e.g., interrupt your interlocutor!), we often miss the rest of the utterance because our brain was busy trying to make sense of what was said earlier.

On a similar note, another difference is that written texts tend to be static, less fluid, and more carefully crafted or edited than oral texts, although that's not always the case. Contrast, for example, a social media post responding to someone in a very casual way and a commercial on TV, which tends to be scripted, rehearsed, and polished.

In case you're wondering . . .

Should we focus more on reading or listening with novice learners? The safest answer would be to strike a balance, but there are several factors to consider in your decision: the students' age, your course or program goals, the students' literacy skills, the level of correspondence between the written and spoken forms of a language, whether the students' native language(s) and the target language use similar scripts or alphabets, etc. We know that people can and do acquire a language entirely aurally, without ever reading or writing anything; at the same time, reading can facilitate acquisition and language development, even if your goals are mainly about oral communication. One thing you should consider incorporating at all levels is bimodal input, which consists of reading and listening at the same time. Bimodal input may help learners in terms of "ear training," and it may also help heritage speakers in terms of making the right phoneme-grapheme connections (i.e., how it sounds and what it looks like written down). There is one caveat about bimodal input that can't be ignored: For some learners, reading and listening at the same time might be too taxing on their attentional resources. In other words, it may be distracting and too much to process. Therefore, if you are going to use bimodal input for texts longer than a couple of sentences, it may be best to use a video as opposed to reading and listening "live" in class. Put learners in control of the speed at which they play the video, allow them to rewind and watch as many times as they need, and give them the option to mute and just read, or close their eyes and just listen.

When it comes to comprehension, word and sentence boundaries tend to be clearer in written texts. For example, if someone says, "your new phone," a learner might divide that utterance into two words: "your" and "nufone," inevitably leading to confusion (i.e., "What is my nufone?). In some cases, cognates might be more easily recognizable in written form, though not always. Furthermore, comprehension of oral texts might be affected by the way the speaker pronounces a word, how loud they talk, and whether there is background noise, music, or overlapping speech, none of which are factors in reading comprehension. Of course, in many cases, we use top-down processing strategies to deduce what we are hearing, based on what we know and expect in that particular context or situation. However, we need to keep in mind that novice and intermediate learners are more likely to rely on bottom-up processes (i.e., they'll want to understand every word to extract meaning) than advanced learners. What do we mean by top-down and bottom-up processes? Funny you should ask! That's what we discuss in the next section.

Selecting Texts

Understanding the processes and factors involved in comprehension of written and oral texts is important for selecting the right texts, which is arguably the hardest part about creating interpretive communication activities. Even though there is some truth to the adage "change the task, not the text," that doesn't mean that any text will do. Both the text and task should be appropriate for the proficiency level of the students.

Let's start with the two processes involved when we encounter a text and try to make sense of it:

- **Top-down processes:** We apply our background knowledge, perspectives, expectations, and experiences to anticipate, understand, and infer ideas.

- **Bottom-up processes:** We extract meaning from the language we encounter by recognizing letters, characters, sounds, words, as well as determining the relationship between the words (e.g., which one is the subject and which one is the object).

Both of these processes play a role in our interpretation of texts. They are not meant to happen in a particular order, and one is not more important than the other. They are equally relevant when it comes to selecting the right text because we should consider these three main factors:

- **Linguistic knowledge:** To what extent are learners able to understand the language of the text (e.g., meaning of words, syntactic relationships, etc.)? Are there cognates and recognizable proper names that may aid comprehension?

- **Background knowledge:** How familiar are learners with the topic, the context, and the purpose of the text? The more we know, the more we can anticipate and deduce.
- **Text features:** Does the text type (e.g., lists vs. paragraph) seem appropriate for the proficiency level of the students? Are there organizational features (e.g., headings and subheadings) or nonlinguistic elements (e.g., pictures, graphs, icons, numbers, gestures, etc.) that may help students understand? In the case of oral texts, speech rate, articulation, and sound quality are also important to consider.

The goal should not be to select texts that will be 100% comprehensible to the learners. It is inevitable (and preferable, actually!) for texts to contain some unknown words. At the same time, if learners are unfamiliar with most of the words in a text, comprehension will be almost impossible, and the whole endeavor won't contribute much, if at all, toward language development. Where's the sweet spot? That depends on what we want students to do with the text. For example, if learners are asked to identify the topic and main idea of a short movie review, they might be able to do so even if they are unfamiliar with several of the words in it. On the other hand, if they are asked to identify in detail which aspects of the movie were positive and negative according to the author of the review, they will need to understand a greater number of words.

In case you're wondering . . .

When watching a video, is it better to use captions (i.e., the transcription) or subtitles (i.e., the translation) to help learners develop listening skills? Research studies on this issue haven't been entirely conclusive, and all of them have limitations, but they seem to indicate that captions are more helpful for listening skills (Birulés-Muntané & Soto-Faraco, 2016), while also facilitating comprehension (Hayati & Mohmedi, 2011). Either way, the learners' proficiency level is a key factor to consider. Captions won't be very helpful if the audiovisual text is too complex for them, and it might actually lead to more confusion due to cognitive overload: too many things to process all at once (Taylor, 2005). This last point underscores the importance of text selection, scaffolding activities, and strategy training. Captioning is not a replacement for any of those; it is simply one more tool.

Although linguistic knowledge has been found to be the strongest predictor of L2 reading comprehension success (Jeon & Yamashita, 2014), it is also important to note that understanding every word within a text is not enough to conclude that learners will be able to adequately interpret it. How much we know about a topic also plays an important role in facilitating comprehension. The way you are reading this chapter is influenced by your experiences, prior knowledge, and expectations: Depending on whether you are an experienced educator or just starting out, you will interpret our ideas and suggestions differently, and you might even retain a different amount of information.

Even though our students differ in their familiarity with various topics, class discussions and activities are shared experiences. Therefore, the texts we choose should be intrinsically connected to and integrated within the corresponding thematic units. If they are, learners will be more likely to understand the language and engage with the content in a deeper, more meaningful way. Furthermore, the topic should be relevant to our students. Is it something they would choose to explore on their own in their native language(s)? Are they learning something that has direct implications for, or connections with, some aspect of their lives? Is the purpose of the text to inspire action on the part of the reader? Are there clear practical applications that might compel learners to want to understand the text? For example, asking learners to create a newscast based on an article they read can be more compelling than merely answering some true/false statements about it.

Reading and Listening Strategies

Can you teach someone how to listen? And if our learners are already literate in at least one language, do we have to teach them how to read in the target language? The answer to both questions is: yes! In fact, research has suggested that training students in how to apply various reading and listening strategies might help increase comprehension (Graham & Macaro, 2008; Kern, 1989; Vandergrift & Tafaghodtari, 2010). However, these strategies don't circumvent all the factors mentioned above when it comes to selecting texts that will be comprehensible to students.

By teaching students various reading and listening strategies, we are giving them tools they can apply on their own later. While it is beneficial to guide them as they put these strategies into action, students shouldn't be forced to approach a text in one particular way. Every reader/listener and every text is different. Plus, we know that readers and listeners don't apply a single strategy when they approach a text: These strategies work in conjunction with one another. Finally, as with everything else involving language teaching, it is not enough to tell students *about* these strategies; we should have learners put these strategies into action.

We can classify strategies into two large categories: local or micro-strategies (i.e., more closely related to bottom-up processes) and global or macro-strategies (i.e., focusing on top-down processes). Striking a balance between these two categories is not easy, and it will depend on the level of the students. Even though our ultimate goal is to focus on understanding main ideas, students at the novice level will need some word-level strategies. After all, you can't understand main ideas if you are not understanding any words!

Local (or micro) strategies:

- Using context to deduce the meaning of words
- Determining when to skip unknown words or phrases
- Previewing or skimming (written texts) based on keywords
- Identifying cognates and other nonlinguistic cues
- Highlighting phrases or words learners understand
- Anticipating language through brainstorming (e.g., mind maps, word clouds)

Global (or macro) strategies:

- Informing yourself about the context of the text and topic
- Diagramming or outlining: identifying main ideas and text organization
- Discussing the topic based on what we already know
- Making predictions based on headings or visual cues
- Anticipating content or organizational features based on prior experiences with similar texts

We will expand on how to put these strategies into action in the next section, but before we do that, let's talk about the first word-level strategy listed above, which tends to be easier said than done: guessing words from context. Without sufficient linguistic knowledge, this strategy may prove to be inadequate, and it can be demotivating for students to guess wrong more often than not. Furthermore, it is not uncommon for context to be insufficient to guess the exact meaning of a word.

What could be a better approach than merely telling students to use context clues? For starters, we can guide learners in the problem-solving process of deducing the meaning of an unknown word. Debriefing and confirming their guesses is an important part of teaching this strategy. If they arrived at the wrong guess, how did that happen? And what could have prevented that? Furthermore, we may want to focus our energy on helping them realize that being able to deduce whether it's an object, a person, or an animal is sometimes good enough to keep reading. In other cases, determining the part of speech (noun, adjective, verb, etc.) is probably sufficient. Of course, as we all know and do when we read in any language, it's perfectly OK to skip some words altogether. For example, do you really need to know what "anfractuous" means in this sentence: "They miraculously managed to cross the anfractuous river"? We are not denying the importance of understanding the meaning of words. After all, we want students to learn new words! However, becoming obsessed with understanding the exact translation of each and every word is something we may want to discourage, especially with novice learners.

Components of Interpretive Communication Lessons

Given what we now understand about the processes and factors involved in comprehension, and assuming we have found a text that is relevant and appropriate for the proficiency level of the students, it's time to plan what to do during each of the major phases in an interpretive communication activity: before, during, and after.

But before we get into the specifics of each phase, we should address the question of whether to keep it all in the target language or to use the shared language. In the case of pre-reading/listening activities, the shared language might be necessary when it comes to developing some of the global strategies we discussed above. Most learners might struggle to understand necessary background information in the target language. However, pre-reading/listening activities should also help learners anticipate what they will encounter in the text, and for that, the target language is necessary. In the case of comprehension questions, the main arguments in favor of using the shared language over the target language are the following:

- Being better able to determine the learners' understanding of the text, as opposed to the questions themselves.
- Ensuring that learners are not merely doing "text matching," where learners scan the text searching for specific words from the questions.
- Engaging in important discussions related to the ideas within the text. As we said in Chapter 2, some topics should not be treated superficially just because learners are unable to discuss them in the target language.

As valid as those reasons are, over-relying on the shared language when learners engage in interpretive activities could also have unintended negative consequences: We might give the wrong impression that understanding a text involves translating it, and it might be difficult to motivate learners to communicate in the target language during other parts of the lesson. However, it doesn't have to be an all-or-nothing choice. Students could answer partly in the shared language and partly in the target language (e.g., using words and phrases from the text).

Pre-Reading/Listening

The overarching goal of pre-reading/listening activities is to facilitate comprehension, and therefore, the pre-reading/listening phase should be as important and elaborate as the post-reading/listening phase. Learners should engage in several activities that help them not only activate prior knowledge, but also anticipate and preview the language they will encounter in the text. Therefore, the pre-reading/listening activities should be specific to the *text* and not just the topic.

Below are some suggestions and tips for creating effective pre-reading/listening activities. Some work better for informational texts, while others are more appropriate for narratives. Teacher discretion is advised.

- Ask questions focused on making connections with content you have been discussing in class, or possibly information students have learned in other classes. You could also have learners inform themselves more about the topic. For instance, if the socio-historical background is necessary to understand a story, the instructor could provide the information, or learners could do some research online (in any language they feel comfortable using).

- Ask questions that establish personal connections with the students' lives, but make sure they are directly related to the text, and not the topic in general. For instance, if the text is about a music festival, it might not be very helpful to ask learners about their favorite artists (i.e., will they mention any of the artists discussed in the text?). And be careful with yes/no questions that might lead to a dead-end. If you ask, "Have you ever been to a music festival?" and some learners say no, you'll need a different strategy!

- Address biases and preconceived notions that may affect the students' interpretation of the text through a "truth or myth" activity.

- Preview and anticipate content by having learners describe images that are directly relevant to the text. In the case of a video, learners could watch part of it with no sound or make predictions based on strategically selected thumbnails of it.

- Have students create drawings based on key sentences or phrases taken from the text.

- Provide the title, topic, and purpose of the text, and ask learners to brainstorm subheadings or subsections they would expect to be included.

- Have learners discuss some of the post-reading/listening questions before they engage with the text. For instance, learners could answer true/false questions prior to reading or listening, based on what they think or know, as we have done at the beginning of each of our chapters. Wording the items in a way that ignites the learners' curiosity to confirm their answers can serve as extra motivation to understand the text.

- Create word-association activities targeting keywords taken from the text to reduce the learners' reliance on dictionary use while they read or listen (e.g., match synonyms and antonyms, spot the odd one out, create word clouds, etc.).

- Prepare activities where learners engage with content that is similar but not identical to that of the text (and modified to their level, if needed). For instance, in the case of narratives, students could put in order a series of events that resemble what happens in the story.

- In the case of oral texts, at least some of the pre-listening activities should focus on phonological-perception skills. For example, the instructor can play a segment of the audio several times, with and without the transcript.

While Reading/Listening

Traditional approaches tend to portray interpretive communication as a passive and individual endeavor. However, having learners engage in activities *while* reading/listening will help them become more active listeners and readers, and thus, get more out of the text. Of course, it's important to make sure the activity doesn't end up being more distracting than helpful (i.e., are we asking learners to do too much at once?). Here are some ideas:

- Break up the text into smaller chunks and have learners pause to summarize, question, reflect, or react. Depending on the type of text, learners could also draw or select a picture that would best illustrate each chunk, make predictions about what will happen next, or offer advice about what the character(s) should do next.

- Have learners complete a graphic organizer where they identify key components of the text (e.g., the characters, the setting, the problem, the sequence of events, and the resolution). In the case of a written text, learners could also highlight information in different colors to indicate the "who," "what," "when," and "why" of the text.

- Reorder scrambled sentences to reassemble a paragraph within a written text.

- Match missing sentences with their corresponding spots within a written text.

- If learners are listening to or watching an interview, have them listen to the responses and deduce what the question was.

- Have learners listen or read once, just to understand keywords, and listen or read again to write main ideas. In groups, learners could share with each other what they understood. Lastly, they should read or listen to the text one more time to confirm the main ideas and add some supporting information.

- Have learners engage in collaborative annotated reading in small groups. This approach will not only help learners appreciate different perspectives on the same text, but also motivate them to come back to it and re-read it.

- After reading a few sentences, have learners write comments (in the shared language) explaining what they think the main idea is, which words they can deduce from context, and which ones they don't think they really need to know. This information can be valuable for the instructor to know what strategies to work on or how to improve the pre-reading/listening activities.

Post-Reading/Listening

Effective post-reading/listening activities should go beyond understanding the main ideas or details. Randi et al. (2005) emphasize the need for a componential approach to comprehension that integrates analytical, practical, and creative abilities. Considering this approach, we offer several suggestions of text-dependent comprehension activities:

- Put events in order or create a timeline.
- Identify inaccurate portions of a summary created by the instructor or other learners (with inaccurate details on purpose!).
- Have learners write a summary with missing keywords, which other learners should complete.
- Select a sentence that would be the best addition to each paragraph. More advanced learners could be tasked with writing one additional sentence for each paragraph.
- Have learners do a free-writing exercise, where they help a classmate who was absent understand what students watched/read in class. Then, have learners compare which ideas and details they included and excluded.
- Create a social media profile for one of the characters based on information disclosed in the text, as well as inferences that can be made about them.
- Other alternatives to explore characters are: writing a text-message exchange between two of them, writing a social media post as one of the characters, or writing an acrostic poem (i.e., the first letter of each line spells out the character's name, and the words describe or are somehow connected to key aspects of the character).
- Making connections within the text and across texts. In addition to the classic prompt about comparing and contrasting ideas expressed by the author, learners could find additional resources and create a thematic collection of texts that reflect a similar point of view as the original text or that share the same communicative purpose and audience (e.g., ads targeting the Latinx market in the United States).
- Establish personal relevance by asking learners to compare the characters to someone they know or make connections between the information presented in the text and their own cultural products, practices, and perspectives.

- Make decisions and suggestions based on the text; for instance, if learners read product reviews, they can indicate which one they would purchase or what other products they would suggest to the authors of the reviews. Similarly, if learners read various job ads, and then listen to different candidates describe their experience and qualifications, they could select the person they would hire and why.
- Write an email to the author or one of the characters; if watching a video, write a comment to post on YouTube.
- Expand the text: come up with an alternative ending, a spin-off story, an additional paragraph or scene, etc. Some learners might find it especially motivating if they can integrate themselves or someone they know (like their teacher!) in the story.
- Have learners speculate how the text would change under different conditions: different narrator, setting, publication year, etc.
- Synthesize and present the information in an alternative format: a brochure, an infographic, a video, a comic strip, or graphic novel, etc. For instance, students could create a poster for the movie adaptation of a story they read.
- Create a board game or video game based on the text.
- Speculate information about the author and the context of the text.
- Ask learners to rewrite or paraphrase certain parts of the text. Doing so will not only help you determine the extent to which they have understood, but it will also prove very useful as a writing skill.
- Complete a modified K-W-L chart, indicating what they already knew (K), what new information they learned (L), and what else they want to know (W) based on the information in the text.

You may have noticed that many of the ideas we listed focus on comprehension at a rather global level, using the text as a springboard for other tasks. This approach doesn't mean that a few true/false items or simple questions aimed at keyword recognition are necessarily bad. In some cases, retrieval of specific information or details is indeed important (or perhaps all the learners can handle!), but we should strive to go beyond that level whenever possible. Otherwise, if *all* of our questions are about specific details from the text, we might be inadvertently encouraging learners to focus on understanding each and every word.

In a nutshell

Before we move on to classroom examples, summarize five main points from this chapter. What are your own takeaways?

_____

_____

_____

_____

_____

Would you like to learn more?
Go to **www.hackettpublishing.com/common-ground-resources**
for a list of suggested readings, webinars, and other resources.

What Does It Look Like in the Classroom?

Example 1: Short Informational Texts (Interpretive Reading)

This example shows the progression of activities that revolve around a short text that summarizes how Christmas and New Year's Day are celebrated in different countries where the target language is spoken. We suggest doing all the activities listed for each section (pre-reading, while reading, and post-reading), but some of the activities could be skipped.

Proficiency level: Novice-high

Pre-Reading

- **Activity 1:** Students match words taken from the text with the corresponding pictures or symbols. Alternatively, the teacher could use a game-based learning platform to ask questions that help students anticipate the vocabulary in the text (e.g., matching words and pictures, spot the odd one out, select the synonym/antonym, etc.).
- **Activity 2:** The teacher provides students with a new list of words or phrases (many of them taken from the text, along with distractors). Students indicate if each one most likely refers to Christmas, New Year's Day, both, or neither. As the teacher reviews their answers, students are reminded that their own cultural practices are influencing their responses, and that for other cultures, the associations might be different.
- **Activity 3:** The teacher asks questions to establish personal connections, while still referencing the content of the text, such as:
  - Are these items used in any celebration in your family?
  - What other symbols, objects, foods, or practices do we associate with these two holidays in our country?

While Reading

- **Activity 1:** Students are told to skim the text and highlight any word from the pre-reading activities.
- **Activity 2:** Students find in the text other possible keywords related to each holiday, even if they are unsure of what the words mean. The teacher writes them on the board and helps students deduce meaning, if possible, or provides them with the translation, a simple

definition in the target language, or a visual representation of it. The class can then decide if it's an important keyword or not.

- **Activity 3:** Students complete a graphic organizer, where they have to write information about foods, practices, colors, etc. by country for each holiday. Not all of the information is provided in the reading, so some of the spots within the graphic organizer are left blank.

Christmas

	Food	Colors	Objects	Practices
Country 1				
Country 2				
Country 3				

New Year's Day

	Food	Colors	Objects	Practices
Country 1				
Country 2				
Country 3				

Post-Reading

- **Activity 1:** Students work in pairs to review and compare their graphic organizers, and they add information if they missed anything; they can also refer to the text if there are any discrepancies.
- **Activity 2:** Students compare their answers to activities #2 and #3 of the pre-reading phase with what the text describes. For example: Are the same objects, foods, or practices associated with those two holidays across cultures?
- **Activity 3:** The teacher displays several images of celebrations around the world; some were described in the text, and others were not. Students select the best images to accompany the text and write the caption for each one.
- **Activity 4:** The teacher provides learners with a series of sentences, each of which could be added to different parts of the original text. Students place the sentences in the corresponding part of the text.
- **Activity 5:** Students use the new information in the supplementary sentences to add to their graphic organizers (e.g., if they didn't have

anything for "food" under "New Year's Day" in a particular country, they can now add it).

- **Activity 6:** Students watch a short video of a person from each of the countries mentioned in the text describing how their family celebrates one of the holidays. The teacher plays the video twice, and the students take notes with respect to similarities and differences between what the person is sharing and the information in the text. The third time the video is played, the teacher stops every so often to confirm whether what was mentioned was similar or different from the written text. As a conclusion, the teacher leads a brief discussion in the shared language about the drawbacks of cultural generalizations and associating a country with a culture.

- **Activity 7 (extension into presentational tasks):** To further demonstrate that culture is not monolithic, but rather, it involves collective and individual layers, students choose a holiday they are familiar with, and they describe how they celebrate it versus how it is typically celebrated. To organize their ideas, they can complete a table like the one below. First, students brainstorm ideas for the first column (i.e., how most people think the holiday is celebrated). Then, individually, students work on the answers for the other two columns. Lastly, the teacher can provide students with some phrases and transition words to help them write a few complete sentences linking their ideas together.

How it is typically celebrated:	Same as how you celebrate it?	Explain differences here:
	Yes / No	
	Yes / No	

Example 2: Back-to-School Commercial (Interpretive Listening)

In this example, the text consists of a commercial for a back-to-school sale in the target language. The ad features a group of children showing some of the items mentioned in the voiceover, but not all of them. This way, the ad offers some visual support, but students still need to understand spoken language to complete the activities.

Proficiency level: Novice-high

Pre-Watching

- **Activity 1:** Students watch part of the video without any sound, and then they make some predictions about the ad. The teacher can facilitate this discussion in the target language by providing choices (e.g., "This ad is probably about . . . (a) a restaurant, (b) a department store, (c) a toy store"). The teacher confirms that the ad is about a back-to-school sale and then asks students to predict what information they think will appear on the ad.

- **Activity 2:** The teacher shows students a printed ad in the target language of back-to-school deals. Students indicate which items in the ad they have in their backpacks that day. The teacher asks students to share their answers and see which items are the most and least popular (i.e., everyone has, or nobody has).

- **Activity 3:** The teacher explains that not everything we have in our backpacks is essential, so to discover the item that students consider to be the most important or essential, the teacher leads students into an input-bracketing activity (see Example 5 of Chapter 3), using items that are mentioned in the commercial students will be viewing.

While Watching

- **Activity 1:** Students are told to listen and try to recognize as many words as they can. After playing the video once, students put a check mark next to the words from the printed ad they heard in the commercial. The teacher plays the video again, and students can add or revise the check marks. In pairs, they compare and confirm what they heard.

- **Activity 2:** Students watch the video again with a listening guide who checks their comprehension of information mentioned in the commercial. The time stamps can be included to help students understand where to listen. For example, some items could be:

  0:30 True or false? The pencils cost $1 for a pack.

  Correct this sentence: The backpack costs $30.

  0:45 When and where is the sale?

  1:00 What are two more details about the sale that you just heard?

Post-Watching

- **Activity 1:** The teacher asks students whether their predictions in the pre-listening activities were correct (e.g., they thought prices would be mentioned, but the ad didn't include any prices), as well as whether the most and least popular items discussed before watching the commercial appeared in it or not.

- **Activity 2:** The teacher provides students with a series of pictures of various items, and students indicate which ones the ad mentioned (i.e., as part of the voiceover). Then, the teacher reads out loud a series of items, and students indicate which ones appeared in the ad (i.e., were shown but not mentioned). The teacher plays the ad one more time so students can confirm their responses.

- **Activity 3:** Students complete a table where they list the supplies that were highlighted in the commercial and add details that they heard about each one (e.g., brand names, colors, etc.). Students then classify the items into the following categories: "I have," "I want," "I don't have or want." Then, the teacher asks a student to read one of their lists without saying which category it is, and the rest of the class guesses if they're referring to items they have, want, or neither.

- **Activity 4:** The teacher reads out loud a series of prices (e.g., "five dollars and fifty cents"), as mentioned in the ad, and the students write each one next to the item (from activity #3) it corresponds to. Once the teacher has confirmed the right prices, students calculate the total cost of the items they wrote in each of the three categories of the previous activity. If appropriate, the teacher can also help students convert the total amount to the currency of the country they live in. The teacher can wrap up the activity by briefly comparing the totals with how much families spend on average on school supplies.

- **Activity 5:** The teacher asks students questions in the shared language about cultural products, practices, and perspectives that are reflected in the commercial (e.g., the images featured on backpacks or folders, the look of the people who appear in the commercial, etc.). Students could also reflect on whether a commercial like that would appear in their own country, and if so, what changes an advertisement agency would make, for instance.

- **Activity 6:** The teacher leads a small discussion about the effectiveness of the commercial in the target language. The students first rate the various parts of the commercial in a chart on a scale of 1 (not effective) to 5 (extremely effective):
  - Images
  - Music/sounds

- ○ Message/words
- ○ Action

Students share their responses, and the class as a whole comes to a consensus on the most effective and least effective aspects. The teacher guides the students to explain why they liked or did not like certain parts of the commercial. Some guiding questions could be:

- ○ Who is the intended audience? Who buys these products?
- ○ What are some important words, actions, and images of the commercial that you saw? Why do you think they were included?
- ○ What is the tone of the commercial: funny, serious, sarcastic, upbeat? What makes you say that?
- ○ What are some things you think the commercial should have included?
- ○ What is the most important phrase from the script?

- **Activity 7 (extension into presentational tasks):** Students work in groups to come up with their own back-to-school commercial, and they act it out using the items in their backpacks. After seeing each "commercial," the audience says which item(s) they would buy. An alternative to the skit can be drawing a storyboard of a commercial. In a storyboard, the students sketch the action within each vignette (as the illustration below) and write the speech bubbles or voiceover script corresponding to each scene. Students could then do a gallery walk and rate the effectiveness of the commercial depicted in one of their classmates' storyboards.

Example 3: Asynchronous Interview (Interpretive Listening)

In this multistep activity, students will be posing questions for a speaker from a country where the target language is spoken, with the goal of guessing which country (and possibly what city) the person is from. Alternatively, the class can be divided up into three or four groups, each of which will be posing questions for a different person. Although it is an "interview," the focus is on interpretive communication since students need to understand the responses of the interviewee to accomplish the task, as opposed to interacting with the person. The students are producing very little or no language on their own.

Proficiency level: Novice-high/intermediate-low

Step 1: The teacher provides students with several choices of questions. Students indicate how helpful each one would be for the task at hand: determining where someone is from. Here are some examples; out of these questions, the last one would not be helpful:

- How big is your city?
- What color is your country's flag?
- How many people live in your city?
- What is a popular sport?
- What is the weather like?
- What are some popular foods?
- When is your birthday?

Step 2 (optional): Students can brainstorm additional questions themselves, with the help of the teacher.

Step 3: Students record short videos reading their questions, and they post them in an online forum that the interviewee can access.

Step 4: The interviewee records a video responding to each of the questions.

Step 5: Students watch the video responses and take notes. Then, each student writes down where they think the person is from by completing these sentences.

I think our guest speaker is from _____.
One reason is _____.
Another reason is _____.
And a third reason is _____.

Step 6: Students compare their answers in small groups and reach a consensus.

Step 7: Groups reveal their guesses, and the teacher confirms if they're right. If possible, students could post additional questions for the interviewee(s) now that they know where they're from.

Step 8 (optional): Students start a K-W-L chart with information that they now know about the country in the first column, which could then be used as part of a pre-reading or pre-listening activity. Alternatively, students can list some misconceptions that they had prior to the conversation and what they learned during the conversation into two columns: before and after the conversation.

Example 4: Animated Legend (Interpretive Listening/Viewing)

The teacher uses an animated video of a legend narrated in the target language. To help students gain a deeper understanding of the legend, the teacher first provides students with pertinent background knowledge. The pre-watching activities also include anticipation of the text structure, language, and content.

Proficiency level: Intermediate-mid/high

Pre-Watching

- **Activity 1:** The teacher explains the background of the community where the legend originated by showing an informational video or providing the students with a short article describing the community. Students answer comprehension questions that focus on information that will be important for students to know so they can have a better understanding of the legend (e.g., what are important crops in the region?).
- **Activity 2:** Students name some legends they are familiar with. Students individually select one of them and complete a graphic organizer indicating the main characters, the setting, the problem, the resolution, and what the legend is meant to explain. Then, the students work in small groups to find elements in common among the legends they selected (e.g., the presence of animals or nature).
- **Activity 3:** The teacher gives students a series of words or short phrases mentioned in the video, written on small strips of paper. Students work in pairs to group the words into one of these categories: person, place, object, description, action.
- **Activity 4:** The teacher shows students thumbnails of various parts of the video and reads out loud a series of sentences from the video.

Students need to match each phrase with the corresponding screen-shot. After the teacher confirms their answers, students guess the order in which the screenshots appear in the video.

While Watching

- **Activity 1:** As students watch the video, they confirm whether the order of the thumbnails predicted in the pre-watching activity was correct. If needed, students can make changes so they have them in the correct order.
- **Activity 2:** The teacher pauses the video halfway through, and the students write a few predictions about how it will end. After they have watched the rest of the video, the teacher briefly asks them how close their predictions were to what actually happened.

Post-Watching

- **Activity 1:** The students create a list of elements that they noticed in both the legend and the video or article from the first pre-watching activity. Then, the class is divided into two or three teams, and each team creates one big list of elements that they all agree on. Each team then reads their list, and if the other teams have the same idea, they scratch it off. The team with the largest number of original examples wins.
- **Activity 2:** Students write sentences that refer to one of the charac-ters (e.g., what they look like, what they do, how they feel, etc.), as well as descriptions of places and objects relevant to the story. They read the statements, and the rest of the class indicates who/what each one describes.
- **Activity 3:** Students write their own summaries of the legend, but some details of it are inaccurate or different from the video. They take turns reading their summaries out loud in small groups, and the other group members need to indicate what parts are different.
- **Activity 4:** Students work in pairs to write five events from the legend onto sticky notes, and another pair of students has to put the sticky notes in the right order on the classroom walls. Then, the class as a whole can organize a larger, more complete timeline on the board combining sticky notes from all of the groups or adding new sticky notes to reflect events none of the groups may have mentioned. The teacher facilitates this process by asking questions such as: "What happens between these two events? What can we add here?"

- **Activity 5 (extension into presentational tasks):** Students work in small groups to come up with a movie or TV series version of the legend. They need to decide what will be adapted and how, as well as which actors would play the roles of the various characters. They also need to write part of the script (e.g., the dialogue within an important scene in their movie) and create the movie poster or trailer.

Example 5: Newspaper Article (Interpretive Reading)

The text for this example is a newspaper article describing a series of protests in a country where the target language is spoken. The topic is connected to information students have been discussing in previous classes. Pre-reading activities help not only to activate and review prior knowledge, but also to anticipate key vocabulary and ideas through discourse scramble.

Proficiency level: Intermediate-high/advanced-low

Pre-Reading

- **Activity 1:** Students complete the "K" and "W" part of a K-W-L chart (know, want to know, learned) individually first and then in pairs to supplement the information they wrote down. The instructor can also help students by prompting them to refer to what was discussed in other units. Students could list any information they know about the country or the protests.
- **Activity 2:** The instructor provides students with a list of word pairs, all of which appear in the article. Students indicate if the pairs are synonyms, antonyms, or neither. In the case of "neither," students can discuss if any other type of relationship exists between the two words.
- **Activity 3:** The instructor provides students with the sentences that make up the first paragraph of the article, but not in the right order. Students reconstruct the paragraph and then write some predictions of what the rest of the article will cover.

While Reading

- **Activity 1:** The instructor provides students with the article scrambled with the paragraphs out of order. The students work to put the paragraphs in order. The teacher verifies the order as a whole class.

- **Activity 2:** Once the students have the paragraphs in the right order, they annotate the article, using symbols to indicate what they already knew (check mark), what parts are new information to them (star), what parts connect to other events or concepts (arrow), and what parts generate new questions for them (question mark). At the end, the students complete these sentences:
  - Something new I learned is: _____.
  - The part about _____ connects to _____ because _____.
  - One question I have is: _____.

Post-Reading

- **Activity 1:** Students fill out the "L" (learned) section on their K-W-L chart. They also confirm whether the questions they wrote under the "W" (want to know) section were answered in the article. Students can do additional research on any unanswered questions and report back to the class.

- **Activity 2:** The instructor provides a series of questions to each group (e.g., "What is one of the consequences of the legislative change explained in the article?"). Students work together to create three options as possible answers, only one of which is correct. Then, groups exchange their multiple-choice questions with another group.

- **Activity 3:** Students do an individual free-writing exercise for five minutes to brainstorm possible connections and comparisons between the protests and other world events or events in their own community. The teacher can provide some questions for students to generate ideas:
  - What are some similar events that have happened in our community or in our country?
  - List three facts that you know about these events.
  - What elements in common do you notice between some of these events?

  Then, in small groups, students discuss their ideas, and then the teacher leads a whole-class discussion, summarizing connections across events, particularly in terms of the social causes behind them.

- **Activity 4 (extension into a presentational task):** Students create an artistic collage or mini-mural reflecting their interpretation of the protests and the social cause behind it. The next class, the teacher posts students' artwork around the room with a blank piece of paper next to each. The students complete a gallery walk, where they observe their classmates' creations and write notes on the blank paper next to each one indicating a symbol they notice and what they think it represents, taking into account what they learned about the event. Students move around the room and continue adding notes to other pieces or writing a different interpretation for symbols that other classmates pointed out. At the end of the gallery walk, the original artists write a reflection on the extent to which their own intentions with each symbol matched the audience's interpretation.

Now That You Know

Discussion and Expansion Questions

1) What similarities and differences can you think of between learning to read in your native language(s) versus an additional language you learned later in life?

2) Think about all the oral and written texts you encounter in your daily life. What types and genres can you list? Which of those are also present in your language classes?

3) Let's analyze these two quotes about reading and listening. For each one, explain what you think the authors meant, and whether the same can be said about the other modality (e.g., if the quote is about reading, could it also apply to listening?).

   a) "Students need to learn to listen so that they can better listen to learn" (Vandergrift, 2004, p. 3).

   b) "The reader drives, the text transports" (Swaffar et al., 1991, p. 74).

4) How do you approach a text in another language? Do you deduce words from context? Do you re-read or listen to a passage more than once? How do you actively engage with the text as you read or listen to it? For example, do you underline words or phrases? Do you take notes?

5) Krashen (1996) argued in favor of narrow listening and reading (i.e., focusing on just one topic, author, or genre), as opposed to exposing learners to different topics and text types within a course. For example, students might only read stories within the Harry Potter series, or they might only read travel blogs. What are some pros and cons of narrow reading and listening, from both practical and pedagogical standpoints? Would the benefits outweigh the drawbacks?

6) There is no reason to doubt the benefits of "free voluntary reading" for language acquisition: When students are able to choose what to read, and they do so voluntarily (i.e., without the obligation of reporting on what they read), they are intrinsically compelled to process language for meaning. Similar programs have also included listening and viewing, so it is not restricted to written texts. However, making it happen in the context of language courses is not always easy. What steps would you need to take to implement "free voluntary reading/listening/viewing" in your classes? What challenges would you anticipate?

7) When we introduced our suggestions and tips for creating effective pre-reading/listening activities, we said that not all worked well for all genres. Go through the list and identify the best activity types for each of these scenarios:

   a) Students will read a short fictional story.

   b) Students will listen to a few people introducing themselves.

   c) Students will watch an interview with a celebrity.

8) One thing conspicuously absent in this chapter is choral reading or any other form of reading aloud. The reason why we excluded it is because there are more drawbacks than benefits to it. Can you think of a few reasons why reading aloud in class might be problematic, particularly when it comes to comprehension? And why do you think choral reading is still alive and well in some language classrooms?

Observation and Application Activities

1) Observe a class of the language you teach, where the students are engaged in an interpretive listening or reading activity. Take notes on the following:

   a) The text: Would you say the text type was appropriate for the students' proficiency level? And what about students' interest in the topic: Could it be something they seek to watch/read outside of class?

   b) Pre-reading/listening activities: How many questions or activities helped students anticipate the language in the text? How many helped them anticipate content/ideas that students would encounter in the text? And how many focused on the topic in general, more broadly?

   c) The students' behavior while reading/listening: Did students approach the text passively or actively?

   d) Post-reading/listening: Did students struggle with any of the comprehension questions? Were there inferencing or cultural connection questions as well?

   e) Use of the target language: Was everything done in the target language, or was the shared language used at any point?

   f) Expansion or connection with other modes: Did students use the ideas in the text as a springboard for other tasks?

2) Choose an interpretive activity from a language textbook and answer the following questions:

    a) Are there pre-reading/listening activities? If so, do they adequately prepare students in terms of both linguistic and background knowledge?

    b) Are there any activities listed for students to complete while reading/listening?

    c) Is the text type appropriate for the students' proficiency level?

    d) Is the topic age-appropriate and interesting to most students for whom the book is intended? Would it be something they seek to watch/read outside of class?

    e) Is comprehension assessed through a variety of activities that go beyond understanding main ideas or details from the text?

3) Select a text that you think would be appropriate and interesting to your students. Create all of the activities that would accompany that lesson:

    a) At least two pre-reading/listening/watching activities that prepare students in terms of both linguistic and background knowledge

    b) One activity for students to complete while reading/listening/watching

    c) At least two post-reading/listening/watching activities that focus not only on comprehension of information and main ideas, but also go beyond the literal (e.g., inferences, comparisons, connections, etc.)

    d) A possible extension into a presentational task

Section III

Presentational and Interpersonal Communication

Chapter 5
Output

Pre-test

Before reading this chapter, indicate whether the following statements are true or false, based on what you know or believe . . . for now!

- The Output Hypothesis posits that producing language is necessary for acquisition.
- Asking students to transform sentences from present to past tense is a form of output.
- Both input and output play important roles in language development.
- Incorporating physical movement might help students in the initial stages of the creative process.
- Corrective feedback on form is not only useless but also detrimental.

Once you have finished, or while you are reading this chapter, verify your answers.

What Do I Need to Know?

Characteristics of Output

Just as we started Chapter 3 by defining what input is, we will start this one by defining **output: producing the target language in order to express meaning**. And, once again: We are not saying merely "language production" because producing sounds or writing symbols without the intention of conveying meaning is not what actually counts as output for language development. In most classrooms, learners are asked to write or say something in the target language quite often (perhaps more often than they should be?), but not all instances count as communicative output, as illustrated in the following table.

What counts as output	What doesn't count as output
Students write a story, and their classmates illustrate it. Then, the class votes for their favorite to be published online so other students can read it.	Students read aloud a short story (i.e., choral reading).
Each student writes five things they did last night. A classmate indicates in what order they probably did them.	The teacher gives learners a list of sentences in present tense. Students rewrite them in past tense.
A student describes a picture, but some of the details are inaccurate (on purpose!). Another student spots the differences by marking the picture while listening to the description.	The teacher reads a vocab list; students repeat each word.
Students create a new course and write a description of it (e.g., topics, assignments, materials, format, etc.). Other students read the description and indicate whether they would take that class, weighing its pros and cons (based on the description).	Students fill in the blanks with the right form of the verbs in parentheses.

The examples in the second column (what doesn't count) can be done without the learners understanding what they're saying or writing. If you made it to Chapter 5 of this book, we probably don't have to work very hard to convince you of why that is problematic.

Now, let's look at this example: "Write a forum post describing your daily routine. Then, read and comment on at least two classmates' routines." Try to answer the two questions we proposed in Chapter 1:

- What information or content is being conveyed?
- What will the audience do with the information?

We know what information is being conveyed, but it's hard to answer the second question for this example because telling students simply to respond is not quite a purpose. A response could potentially be something generic like "I like your routine," even if the student didn't understand most of what their classmate wrote. And why do students have to respond to at least two classmates, other than just because they were told to do so?

By contrast, you would indeed be able to answer both questions for all the scenarios of the first column (what counts). Students are **compelled** to express **meaning**. If this message is starting to sound familiar, then you're getting it!

Now that it's clear what we mean by output, let's discuss its role in language development.

The Output Hypothesis

In the mid-1980s, when Krashen's Monitor Model was all the rage, Merrill Swain questioned the part about input being sufficient for acquisition. Her evidence came from Canadian immersion programs, where learners seemed to attain native-like comprehension skills thanks to years of input-rich instruction, and yet, they appeared to be lagging behind in their production abilities.

The Output Hypothesis (Swain, 1985) proposes that the processes in which learners engage when "pushed" to produce an accurate and meaningful message are facilitative of language development because it helps them pay more attention to linguistic form. Specifically, Swain suggested that output helps learners notice or realize what they do not know, and as they fill those gaps in their knowledge, their language develops.

Let's pause and think about the following: How do they fill those gaps? Isn't that benefit of output actually tied to input? Indeed, Swain acknowledged that when learners realize they don't know how to say something they want to express, they will seek a solution "by turning to a dictionary or grammar book, by asking their peers or teachers, or by noting to themselves to pay attention to future relevant input" (Swain, 2000, p. 100). It doesn't work as efficiently as that quote makes it sound, but the point is: Without input, none of those gaps would be filled. In other words, output might help learners realize what they need *from the input*, and in that sense, you could say that it is facilitative of language acquisition. But when we produce language, we are accessing the system, not adding to it. Output doesn't build the system; only input does, and that is why Krashen maintained that input was *sufficient* for *acquisition* (i.e., for building the system).

It's important to clarify that the notion of "pushing" learners to produce accurate (or, at least, more precise) messages was not meant to imply that learners should be forced to talk and write perfectly from day 1 or that teachers should demand perfection in every utterance. In fact, that would do more harm than good since it would likely inhibit students' willingness to produce anything or make them worry so much about accuracy that their fluency would be thwarted.

Swain also viewed output as a way for learners to test hypotheses about the target language: They try things out and, based on feedback, they confirm or reject those hypotheses. We'll come back to the role of interactional feedback in the next chapter. For now, let's focus on the idea that expressing meaning triggers certain processes that may facilitate language development, which is essentially what the Output Hypothesis is all about.

The Role of Output

Keating (2016) provides the clearest description of the role of output in language development: "Output hones a learner's ability to access the implicit system with accuracy and speed" (p. 22). If our goal is to help learners develop communicative ability in the target language, then both input and output should have a place in our curriculum because they play important, yet different, roles in language acquisition and development: One builds the linguistic system, and the other helps with the skill of accessing that system.

In other words, there is no need to declare whether you are "Team Krashen" or "Team Swain." Saying that input is necessary doesn't mean output is unnecessary. Of course, when it comes to teaching novice learners, if we are dedicating more time to output than input, then something is not right. How can you develop the skill of accessing a linguistic system when there have been little opportunities to develop it in the first place?

Unfortunately, most introductory-level textbooks still reflect an obsession with output. Many more activities per chapter are all about getting learners to produce language, as opposed to engaging in comprehension of meaningful messages. Why? Probably because some educators associate input with something passive and teacher-centered, whereas output feels more active and learner-centered, which are two words that tend to describe "good teaching." Plus, many people continue to associate communication with speaking or writing (i.e., producing language, sending a message), when in reality, comprehension is also communication.

In case you're wondering . . .

How much input do students need before you can move to output? Unfortunately, there is no magic formula or number we can give you. Unlike babies learning their native language(s), our students will likely start producing language on their own soon after being exposed to the language, whether we want them to or not, though some learners might need more time than others. Instead of focusing on quantifying the exact ratio of input and output, we would simply recommend focusing on providing learners with copious opportunities to engage meaningfully with the language, while being aware of what learners can do and need at their proficiency level. For instance, we know that novice learners have a long way to go when it comes to developing a linguistic system in their heads, so they will need considerably more input than output. That being said, controlled or limited output can still have a place and a role in novice-level classrooms.

Process versus Product

When someone brings up presentational communication, most people think of the final product: a double-spaced composition or a student presenting in front of a class. That's the destination, but how do students get there? Providing them with a prompt like "create a 10-minute presentation on X country" or "write a 150-word paragraph about X topic" is clearly not enough because it is still focused on the end-result. It's the equivalent of giving someone an address without directions or a GPS.

Successful presentational communication is planned and organized, and to get there, we all go through a *process* of crafting a message. We can minimally name the following three aspects of the presentational communication process, which is the consensus among writing researchers (e.g., Flower & Hayes, 1981):

- **Planning:** generating ideas, deciding on content organization
- **Drafting:** putting ideas on paper, so to speak
- **Revising:** expanding, eliminating, modifying, etc. Revisions can be made at the surface level (e.g., editing language) or at a more global level (e.g., reorganizing content).

Even though most presentational writing activities make it seem as though these phases happen consecutively (i.e., first, brainstorm; then start writing; and, finally, revise), we know that writers engage in all phases continuously and cyclically. You might start by generating an outline, then start drafting part of it and revising as you draft, and then you might decide to eliminate some of your original ideas and generate others, reorganize the content based on these newly generated ideas, draft some more, revise as you write, etc. Something very similar can be applied to presentational speaking: You certainly plan what you want to say, craft an initial presentation, select visual aids, revise as you put ideas on your slides, etc.

Scaffolding the Process

We all have our own way of approaching a presentational task: We don't all follow the same process. However, that doesn't mean learners are on their own. There are several things we can do to help students successfully convey their messages.

First, students should not be expected to engage in a specific type of presentational communication without having had the chance to see good models of it. Moving from input to output applies to all aspects of a lesson. When it comes to writing, in particular, the more we read, the better we write. It's not about copying, but rather about being inspired by what we read, in addition to gaining a better understanding of different genres. For example, if you want your students to write a review of a restaurant, it won't help them much to read menus. Instead, at least one of the interpretive reading components of that lesson should indeed involve restaurant reviews.

Second, the instructions themselves should emphasize the process over the product. At the risk of sounding like a broken record, if the instructions or prompt consist only of a topic ("write about X") with specific requirements and a single deadline, then we are sending the message that all we care about is the final product. Instead, learners should work on writing assignments a little at a time, with separate deadlines for separate steps. Help learners see the value of stepping away from their own writing for a while and coming back to it with fresh eyes. And, yes, that applies to all writing assignments, no matter how short.

Third, have students reflect on the idiosyncrasies of their own process so they become aware of what works best for them. For instance, do they write with music on or in silence? Do they move around when they feel stuck and can't think of what else to say? What time of day do they feel more inclined to write? Is there a particular space where they're more comfortable (e.g., inside or outside)? What about handwriting versus typing? We all have our preferences, but not everyone is aware of them. One way you can help them reflect on their writing process is to have them draw it or keep a journal (in any language they feel comfortable with) as they complete a writing task.

Last but not least, don't forget about the audience and its role, which in turn will help to make the purpose for writing clear and concrete. In the language classroom, the audience is usually the teacher or other learners. When the audience is other learners, we should think of output as helping to provide input for them, and therefore, it should be clear what the other students need to do with that information. When the audience is the teacher, we tend to think of writing as a way for us to evaluate students' language skills. Although there is nothing wrong with using writing tasks as formative or summative assessments, we should still focus on having learners communicate something meaningful to us (i.e., asking learners to tell us, in writing, something we want to know).

In case you're wondering . . .

Could online translators be helpful for students to complete writing assignments? For some language teachers, using online translators constitutes a form of cheating (or unauthorized assistance), whereas others have come to accept and invite their presence into the classroom. While it is true that bilingual professionals use online tools in the real world, we can probably agree that they did not develop a high level of communicative ability by using translators. There is no evidence that copy-pasting what Google said fosters language development. In fact, we could argue that it is a way of bypassing learning. We don't deny the potential usefulness of online translators for advanced and superior-level speakers, but most language educators teach novice and intermediate learners, so let's focus on that. First, we need to make sure that every aspect of our instructional practices is in line with what we know about second language acquisition and proficiency levels. Are we being realistic about what we are aiming for? Are we moving too quickly from input to output? Have we adequately prepared students to do the task at hand? Proper scaffolding, as opposed to having students "write 100 words on X topic," can help to minimize students' inclination to rely entirely on an online translator. It is important to recognize that even if we have done everything right pedagogically, some students will resort to online translators to complete the simplest of assignments, merely for convenience. Henshaw (2020) outlines some course modifications that could help to dissuade online translator use.

Helping Learners Generate Ideas

Typically, students struggle the most with the initial stages of the writing process: planning what to write or generating ideas. Many of the suggestions out there resemble some of the pre-reading activities we discussed in Chapter 4: graphic organizers, word associations, answering questions, etc. Another way of helping students generate ideas is to incorporate movement, if possible (e.g., letting students walk around the classroom for a minute while they think about what to write). And as we mentioned before, interpretive communication can indeed play an important role in generating ideas toward a presentational task.

A well-known strategy to help learners overcome the fear of facing a blank page is to engage in frequent free-writing exercises, where learners write everything as it comes to them for a certain amount of time, nonstop. Although it certainly may help some learners at the intermediate level (and up!) get more comfortable letting their ideas flow, novice learners would likely find free writing in the target language to be a frustrating experience. Instead, provide them with simple questions or sentence starters.

WWW.PHDCOMICS.COM

Helping Learners Revise Their Writing

An important component of the writing process is feedback, and yet, this task is probably the most time-consuming (and neuron-consuming!) one for teachers. We are all about making the best use of our time while maximizing language development, so we need to confront head-on the question of the usefulness of feedback on writing. Despite abundant research, it is difficult to find an obvious, clear trend since not all feedback is created equal: content versus form, focused versus unfocused, etc. Although feedback on global issues (organization, clarity of ideas, etc.) is an important topic, we feel it goes beyond the scope of this book. Thus, in this section, we will only discuss the merits, if any, of form-focused feedback. Haven't we all wondered whether correcting errors on students' papers is worth our time?

On the one hand, Truscott (1996) posited that "grammar correction has no place in writing classes and should be abandoned" (p. 361). One of the reasons against corrective written feedback is that we are sacrificing meaning in the name of accuracy. The teacher seems much more concerned about accuracy than the message being conveyed (i.e., do we care about what the students are telling us?), which can not only be demotivating to the students, but also make them simplify their output and stick to what they know will be correct. Another argument is that any effects we might see are usually temporary and only "pseudo learning," according to Truscott (1996): A student might change a particular form based on the instructor's correction, but that doesn't mean students have now acquired or learned the "correct" form.

On the other hand, Ferris (1999) asserted that "effective error correction—that which is selective, prioritized, and clear—can and does help at least some student writers" (p. 4). A lot of the reasons in favor of error correction stem from the premise that conscious attention to form is facilitative of language development, and not everyone agrees with that premise. Also, did you notice all of the disclaimers and caution in the quote above? Even the pro-feedback camp admits that certain conditions need to be met for feedback to be helpful, and even then, there are no guarantees of its effectiveness. Some of the conditions can be somewhat controlled by the teacher; for example, students should do something with the feedback, other than simply looking at it. If you are giving them feedback without any immediate need to use it, then it is probably not worth your time and effort.

In case you're wondering . . .

Is peer feedback as effective as instructor feedback? Well, that is not a fair comparison. Would you really be surprised if we told you that students tend to prefer and trust instructor feedback more than suggestions from their peers? The real question is: What benefits does peer feedback have, and do they outweigh the drawbacks (e.g., mistrust, inadequate suggestions, etc.)? Research so far suggests that peer feedback may indeed be valuable for both the giver and the receiver, although its usefulness appears to be dependent upon the attitude or disposition of the learners and how well they work together (Storch & Aldosari, 2019). This is yet another reminder that we should foster collaboration throughout the process (not just at the end), and we should have students work with a variety of partners. The one thing that just about all L2 writing scholars agree on is that peer feedback requires scaffolding, training, and instructor intervention. In other words, we can't simply tell students to give each other feedback and hope for the best. It is certainly not a replacement for instructor guidance. In fact, incorporating peer feedback in the writing process does not mean "less work" for the instructor, but it might actually imply more work in the form of carefully structuring the peer-feedback activity and assisting peers as they work together.

Here's where things get tricky . . . or trickier. Research has shown that correcting a little bit of everything (i.e., unfocused feedback) does not really work, which is why Ferris uses the adjectives "selective" and "prioritized." How do we know which forms to focus on so that we give feedback efficiently? That is as hard to predict as being able to tell exactly what does and does not get acquired from the input. All we can tell you is that it has nothing to do with whatever you have "covered" in class or the current textbook chapter. Given how difficult—if not impossible—it is for teachers to know exactly how to provide the right feedback at the right moment for each and every student, it is not surprising that any observable effects are limited at best.

Perhaps the only thing most experts agree on when it comes to feedback is that it may contribute to explicit knowledge, which may be useful for future monitored production. But here's the fine print: "we have not sorted out what explicit knowledge students can and cannot apply, and all teachers know that students do not apply all of their explicit knowledge when writing or editing" (Polio, 2012, p. 386).

All in all, the takeaway message is: Curb your enthusiasm and expectations. We are not saying that feedback won't ever do anyone any good, and we certainly do not agree that all feedback is detrimental or harmful (sorry, Truscott!), but at the same time, we know that corrective feedback is not a magic cure for all language errors, it won't be helpful for all learners, and its effects might not be immediate or even sustained. Also, as Ferris (1999) said, the feedback needs to be clear. Telling students just to be careful with verb conjugations, for instance, is too vague, and it will likely not have much of an effect other than diminish their confidence in their language skills. Equally important is to avoid using metalinguistic jargon (e.g., "accusative case," "gerunds," "past participles," etc.) since most learners won't know what to do with that information, even if they are terms you have used in class.

In addition to having realistic expectations when it comes to the effects (if any!) of feedback, what we expect in terms of *accuracy* should be in line with the students' proficiency level: Novice and intermediate learners require a sympathetic interlocutor, rather than a red pen. Instead of focusing so much on whether we are providing enough corrective feedback, it might be best to focus on whether we are providing enough opportunities to engage meaningfully and purposefully with language. Focus on what learners are sharing with you (content, ideas), and respond with meaningful messages (input) back to them. Granted, some errors might genuinely create a breakdown in communication, and, in those cases, it would be helpful to ask for or provide some clarification.

In a nutshell

Before we move on to classroom examples, summarize five main points from this chapter. What are your own takeaways?

_____

_____

_____

_____

_____

Would you like to learn more?
Go to **www.hackettpublishing.com/common-ground-resources**
for a list of suggested readings, webinars, and other resources.

What Does It Look Like in the Classroom?

Example 1: Animated Video (Presentational Speaking)

In this example, students create an animated video with pictures, words, and background music. The theme of the video is "Top five tips for . . .," which lends itself to list-like production, and thus, it is appropriate for novice learners. The first activities in the sequence provide learners with a model to emulate. Even though the format is different (i.e., an infographic versus a video), the text type and objective are the same. In this example, students help to choose the topic that will be assigned to the entire class; alternatively, students could work in small groups and select their own subtopic within a thematic unit.

Proficiency level: Novice-high

Step 1: Students read an infographic summarizing "five ways to protect the environment," and they rank the tips from most important to least important. They compare their rankings in small groups and come to a consensus. Then, they write a new tip to replace the least important one.

Step 2: The teacher guides the students in noting certain things about the text, such as the length of the utterances, whether the author has included things to do or to avoid, and words that might be useful when giving tips to someone.

Step 3: Students brainstorm specific topics, all related to the theme "top five tips." First, they work in pairs to come up with as many possibilities as they can, guided by the question "top five tips for what?" Then, the teacher writes several options on the board as students share them (e.g., "for doing well in class," "for helping our community," "for new students in our school," etc.). The class votes to decide what the topic will be.

Step 4: Students work individually to generate ideas and brainstorm words associated with that topic. If needed, students can look up words that they don't know. Each student writes a list with 10 tips. They exchange their lists with a classmate and mark which tips they have in common; for any that are different, they rank them according to how important or good they think the tip is.

Step 5: The teacher asks each pair of students to share one tip on the board. They cannot share the same tip as another group. If needed, the teacher can provide feedback on the tips that students wrote on the board, particularly to increase comprehensibility.

Step 6: Each student now finalizes their own list of five tips and creates a video, where the tips are ranked in order of importance.

Step 7: Students share their videos in an online discussion forum. Their classmates watch a classmate's video and indicate how their tips and ranking are similar or different from the ones in their own videos. Alternatively, the teacher can select a few videos to play in class and have students note similarities and differences.

Step 8 (optional): Students could vote for their favorite videos, and those could be shared publicly, such as on the school's social media pages, provided that the videos are anonymous. This could be a particularly great option if the topic is related to their own school or community.

Example 2: Texting Dialogues (Presentational Writing)

In this example, students will write a text-message conversation between two celebrities or characters. Since most text conversations consist of straightforward exchanges of information in the form of phrases and sentence fragments, this example works well for novice-level students. Even though it is a "dialogue," it is not interpersonal communication because there is no interaction: Each student is individually writing the conversation as if it were a script.

Proficiency level: Novice-high

Step 1: The teacher presents a list of "SMS" abbreviations that are common when two speakers of the target language communicate via text message. Students match each abbreviation with the corresponding word or phrase. For instance:

1)	ttyl	a)	Thanks
2)	thx	b)	Talk to you later
3)	idk	c)	Saturday
4)	Sat	d)	I don't know

Step 2: Students read a text conversation that the teacher has written between two celebrities discussing their weekend plans, like the one on the following page. Alternatively, the conversation can be about other topics, depending on the unit.

As they read, students complete the chart below with information from the conversation. If something is not mentioned, they write "idk." Then, the class reviews the answers and comes up with possible alternatives for the spots where they wrote "idk."

	Seeing a movie	Baseball game	Dinner
When?			
Where?			
With whom?			

Step 3: Students brainstorm a list of their favorite characters/celebrities as a class, as well as several activities that each of those people enjoys doing. The class decides on two characters/celebrities that they want to write about from the brainstorm list and fill out a similar chart with ideas they can include in the conversation.

	(activity)	(activity)	(activity)
When?			
Where?			
With whom?			

Step 4: Each student writes a texting conversation between the two characters/celebrities, following the model in Step 2 and using ideas from Step 3.

Step 5: Students exchange their text conversation with a partner, who reads it and adds appropriate emojis in different parts of the conversation.

Example 3: Class Mascot Pitch (Presentational Writing)

This example is similar to a business pitch but adapted for younger learners. Each student nominates a class mascot to represent their class. It can be a real animal or a fantasy animal (i.e., a mash-up of different animals). First, the teacher provides a model not only to help learners understand the task at hand, but also to provide words and expressions that students can use in their own pitches.

Proficiency level: Novice-high/intermediate-low

Step 1: The teacher describes a school mascot (e.g., the mascot of the teacher's alma mater), and students draw it. The teacher later displays the actual image, and students can compare their drawings to it. Then, the teacher explains that students will be creating their own mascot to represent their class.

Step 2: The teacher facilitates a short brainstorming session, similar to the one described in Example 4 of Chapter 1, to help students generate ideas and have the language necessary to write their own descriptions.

Step 3: Students individually write their descriptions. The teacher walks around and helps them. As students ask for help with specific words, the teacher writes them on the board, not only in case other students have the same question, but also because it would facilitate comprehension for the next step.

Step 4: Students pair up: One student reads what they wrote, and the other draws the mascot based on the description. Then, they switch roles. At the end, they look at what their partners drew, and if any part of the drawing doesn't match the description, students work to make changes.

Step 5: Students display their final drawing and description. Students write down their top three favorites in secret and turn them in to the teacher. The teacher tallies the top votes and announces which one will be the class mascot. This way, students do not know how many votes each one received. Alternatively, to completely eliminate competition, the teacher can collect the drawings and descriptions, and then the next class, the teacher posts the drawings around the classroom, reads the descriptions aloud, and students have to point to the right drawing.

Example 4: For Sale (Presentational Writing)

In this example, students write a description of an item for sale (clothes, old toys, collectibles, furniture etc.). As always, the teacher begins by providing models for students not only to understand what is expected but also to activate some of the linguistic knowledge needed to complete the task. This activity works best as part of an online discussion forum where students can read what others have posted and respond. Alternatively, it could be done as a gallery walk in class, where the "ads" are posted on the classroom walls and the students circulate reading them and commenting on them.

Proficiency level: Novice-high/intermediate-low

Step 1: Students read five descriptions of items for sale online (written by the instructor or found online and modified, if necessary). They match each description with the picture of the item, as well as its price. The teacher verifies their answers.

Step 2: The teacher asks students to identify what information is included in the ads they read in Step 1. Then, the class as a whole creates a list of words and phrases that they could use in their own ads.

Step 3: Individually, students choose an item to sell and jot down some ideas (bullet points) of what to include in their ad. All students are told not to include the price of the item. The teacher walks around the room and offers assistance, as needed.

Step 4: Students share their ideas in small groups. Their classmates ask questions about the item so the seller knows what additional information to include.

Step 5: Students finish writing their ads and post them in an online discussion forum. Their classmates write comments indicating how much they would pay for the item based on the description.

Step 6: The sellers respond to the comments by indicating whether they would be willing to sell their item for any of the prices offered by their classmates.

Example 5: Fan Fiction (Presentational Writing)

This example explains an idea for incorporating scaffolded creative writing into lower-level courses. The starting point is another text students have engaged with in class (e.g., a movie, TV series, or reading a story or novel). In this example, students are creating a new story after modifying certain parts of the original.

However, other possibilities for fan fiction could be extending the story, changing how it ends, or rewriting it for a different time period.

Proficiency level: Intermediate-low

Step 1: In pairs, students brainstorm as many details about the original story as they can remember. Students can write the list in present tense, for instance:

- Main characters: John and his dog
- The dog is brown
- John is 10 years old
- They live in Sleepy Creek
- Small house

Then, each pair shares with the class the details they listed, and if no other group included it in their lists, the pair gets a point. The pair with the most points at the end is declared the winner. When a group shares a piece of information that all the other groups also listed, the teacher writes it on the board.

Step 2: Using all the details mentioned, the teacher leads the whole class in a review of the original storyline by asking questions such as: Where does the story start? What happens next? Why does he feel sad?

Step 3: The teacher explains that they will be writing a new version of the story but changing all of the details compiled on the board. In small groups, students brainstorm possible alternatives. For instance, if all groups in Step 1 listed where the story took place, they now come up with a new setting.

Step 4: Individually, students start rewriting the story with the new details. First, they can write a bullet-point list combining the events of the original story and the new details. As students are working, the teacher walks around and helps them, as needed.

Step 5: Students transfer their bullet-point notes onto a new piece of paper, but this time, aiming to write complete sentences and adding more details. Students submit their rough draft to the teacher for feedback.

Step 6: The students make revisions based on the teacher's feedback, and they create illustrated books of their new stories, which can be read by next year's students.

Example 6: Mini-Research Study (Presentational Speaking)

In this example, students collect data through a survey and summarize their results in an oral presentation, which can be extended into a presentational writing task. An assignment like this one can be tailored to any topic, and the type of data learners collect can also be adapted to the students' circumstances and opportunities (e.g., if they only have access to other students within their own school or if they can reach out to others online). It works best with high school and college students. Unlike more traditional research presentations, where students essentially summarize information found online, this task gives learners ownership of the information they are presenting and helps them understand the basics of conducting data-driven research.

Proficiency level: Intermediate-mid

Step 1: The teacher gives a mini-research presentation to the class, as a model, on a topic that would be of interest to the students (e.g., "is there a relationship between our favorite colors and our personality?"). As the students listen to the presentation, they fill out a graphic organizer where they take notes on the following six parts of the presentation:

- Introduction/background info
- Research questions
- Participants
- Survey
- Results
- Conclusion

Step 2: At the end of the presentation, students work in groups to add information and details to their graphic organizers. Then, the teacher asks some comprehension questions about the content of the presentation.

Step 3: Students work in pairs to brainstorm and decide on a topic that they will research, which should be connected to topics discussed in the course (e.g., healthy habits, pastimes, travel preferences, opinions on current events, etc.). When they have decided on a general topic, they are prompted to write their research question(s): What do they want to find out? The teacher provides examples, such as:

- "What motivates students to continue studying Spanish after the second year?"
- "Is there a relationship between our pastimes and our career goals?"

Step 4: Students inform themselves on the topic by searching for information online in any language they are comfortable with, as well as consulting with the instructor, and then, they outline some key terms to define in their introduction (e.g., intrinsic and extrinsic motivation).

Step 5: Students write the questions to include in their survey. Depending on the topic and who will be completing the survey, the questions would need to be in the target language or the shared language. First, they write some demographic questions (e.g., age, year in school, languages spoken, etc.) to better understand their participants' background. Then, they write the items or questions that would help them answer their research questions. Students should write no more than 10 multiple-choice or Likert-scale items, and no more than two open-ended items. The teacher can assist groups that are struggling to come up with questions.

Step 6: Students exchange the draft of their survey with another group, who gives them feedback on how clear the questions are and offers suggestions about additional items they could include or anything else they should revise.

Step 7: Students create the survey online, and they share it with potential participants, who could be other students, teachers, friends, family members, etc., depending on what learners are researching. The teacher provides a deadline by which students must have at least 10 responses.

Step 8: Students summarize the characteristics of their participants based on information provided in the survey, as well as the trends they found in the responses they collected. Then, they draw some conclusions that serve as answers to their research question(s).

Step 9: Students put together a presentation, which should have the following sections:

- Introduction/background info
- Research questions
- Participants
- Survey
- Results
- Conclusion

Step 10: Each group presents their findings to the class. For each presentation, the audience is instructed to do the following:

- After the group presents their research question(s), the audience members should write some predictions about what they think the group found.

- At the end of the presentation, the audience members should indicate if their predictions were right. Then, they should propose a new idea or additional question related to the topic (i.e., what else would they want to find out about it?).

Example 7: Interactive Fiction (Presentational Writing)

This example combines fan fiction and interactive fiction. Students will be extending a story (from a reading or movie) they have previously explored in class by creating a "choose your own adventure" version of it, where the readers essentially decide the fate of the characters through a series of choices. Parts of the story resemble the original reading or movie, while others are new. The interactive-fiction story could also be entirely new and based on one of the characters from the original story, like a sitcom spin-off. Alternatively, students could create a digital audio book (with one story line) instead of an interactive-fiction story.

Proficiency level: Intermediate-mid/high

Step 1: Students summarize the events of the original story, and they identify points where the characters could face a dilemma or need to make a binary choice. For instance:

> John woke up and rode his bike to school (original story).
> John woke up, and started to ride his bike to school, but then he saw a dog running loose. What did John do?
> Option A: continued riding his bike to school.
> Option B: started following the dog.

To keep track of the different story lines, students create a story map, like the following:

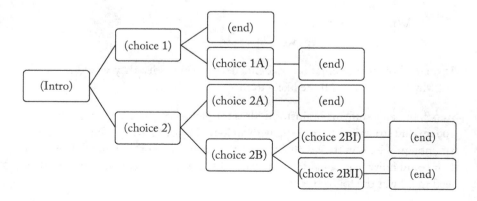

Step 2: Students give each other peer feedback on the story lines and decisions. They can verify that the original story line still makes sense and suggest alternatives or additional details for the new parts.

Step 3: Once the story map is finalized, students can start writing each portion of the story. Their first draft should focus on the actions. Then, the teacher can provide feedback and suggest ways to add details and richness to the story. Students can expand what they wrote based on their instructor's suggestions and then get additional feedback from their peers (someone different from Step 2).

Step 4: Students work in pairs to illustrate each other's stories. They read each part and find or draw an image to go with it.

Step 5: Students publish their illustrated interactive-fiction story online so other students can read it. If other classmates are reading them, they can share with the class how their version of the story ended based on their choices.

Example 8: Business or Product Pitch (Presentational Speaking)

In this example, students come up with a new business or product idea, and then create a presentation to convince the audience to "invest" in their company. Alternatively, students could pitch an idea for a new community organization or club in their school.

Proficiency level: Intermediate-mid

Step 1: The teacher gives a presentation on two different ideas. The first idea is a matchmaking service for would-be pet owners and pets; the second idea is a buffet-style restaurant where people pay for their food by weight. The presentation of each idea is organized around the following three sections:

- Why there is a need for it
- What the business entails
- How the investment would be used

At the end of the presentation, students decide which idea they would invest in, and why they think it is more likely to succeed.

Step 2: In pairs, students brainstorm ideas for their own businesses or products. If students are struggling to come up with an idea, they can start by identifying some common problems in their daily life (e.g., time management) or potential needs in their community (e.g., an indoor dog park). Once they have chosen one idea, they need to answer the following questions:

- What problem does it solve, or what benefits does it provide?
- How does it work? What does it do or offer?
- What steps should be taken to implement it, and how will the investment help?

Step 3: As students work on the three sections of their presentation (i.e., the same ones as in Step 1), the instructor meets with each group and provides feedback on their ideas, content, and language.

Step 4: Students create a name and a logo for their business, which they include in the title slide. They also plan who will talk about what during their presentation.

Step 5: Students pitch their ideas. Each student chooses five of those ideas they would invest in, and why they think they are likely to succeed.

Example 9: Study Abroad Essay (Presentational Writing)

This example shows a process approach to writing a personal essay that most college students are expected to submit along with their study-abroad application materials. Even though the students' proficiency level is higher than in other examples, the process still starts with reading. Once students have a good idea of what is expected, the planning phase begins. Peer and instructor feedback are incorporated throughout: Peers help each other with generating ideas; the instructor helps polish them up. Although the final product is important, the bulk of the work lies in the multiple steps that lead up to it.

Proficiency level: Intermediate-high/advanced-low

Step 1: Students read a sample essay that serves as a good model for what they need to write. First, the instructor asks questions to guide students in recognizing what information the author included, particularly about their interest in the program and their ability to adjust to the challenges of living in another country. Then, students use the following rubric to evaluate the essay, rating their agreement with each statement on a scale of 1 to 5:

- Each paragraph presents a different idea that helps to convey why the student would be a good fit for the chosen program.
- Supporting examples from personal experiences are developed thoroughly with specific details.
- The information within each paragraph is cohesive.
- The essay is organized in a logical and clear manner, making good use of transition words to guide the reader.

In groups, students discuss and compare their ratings for each statement. In cases of disagreement, students need to explain their scores. In cases where a score lower than 5 was assigned, students make suggestions for improvement.

Step 2: Students look for information about study-abroad programs in their institution and then select two they would be interested in.

Step 3: In pairs, students share with each other which programs they selected and why. They also work together to write a pros/cons list for each program to help them decide which one of the two they like best.

Step 4: Individually, students do a free-writing exercise for about eight minutes. They write everything they can think of concerning why they want to participate in that particular program, with emphasis on how it will help them achieve their academic and professional goals. Once time is up, students are told to read what they wrote and make any desired changes (e.g., adding, deleting, reorganizing). Then, they post what they wrote on an online discussion forum.

Step 5: Each student is assigned a new classmate (different from Step 3) to read and comment on their post. Comments should include: what they like the most about the student's paragraph, what parts contain vague or generic statements (i.e., can anything be applied to any program at all?), and to what extent the student successfully explains how this study-abroad program in particular relates to their academic interests. If needed, they can suggest ways in which the student can include or expand that part. Once comments are posted, the original student makes revisions in light of their feedback.

Step 6: In groups of three, students brainstorm and discuss what challenges they might face while living abroad, as well as experiences they have had that could serve as good examples of how they would handle difficult situations abroad. Ideally, groups should be formed according to the program or location students chose.

Step 7: Individually, students do a free-writing exercise for about eight minutes. They write everything they can think of about the challenges of living abroad and how they would be able to handle those challenges through specific examples or experiences.

Step 8: Using the ideas they discussed and wrote about in class, students write a first draft of their personal essay at home, addressing the following two aspects:

- Connections between the program they chose and their academic/professional interests and goals
- Challenges and opportunities of living abroad, including at least one personal experience that demonstrates adaptability and resourcefulness

Step 9: The instructor reads the students' drafts and provides written comments on areas of strength, as well as parts that may need to be expanded or revised.

Step 10: Students are given time in class to look at the instructor's feedback and make changes. If students need help understanding the instructor's comments, they can ask for clarification.

Step 11: Students work on writing a revised and expanded version at home. They are told to write down any questions that come up as they continue writing.

Step 12: The instructor meets individually with each student the week prior to submitting the final version. These one-on-one consultations provide students with an opportunity to get their questions answered and receive help on specific aspects of their essay before putting the finishing touches on it.

Step 13: Students submit the final version, which is graded holistically.

Now That You Know

Discussion and Expansion Questions

1) VanPatten (2003) said that output may help learners "be better processors of input" (p. 69). How do you interpret that quote based on what you now know about the role of output?

2) When Swain proposed the Output Hypothesis, she included metalinguistic reflection as one of the benefits of producing language, which essentially consists of learners consciously reflecting on the language itself as they monitor their production. For example, while writing, a learner might stop and wonder if they need to use the prepositions "in" or "on." Consider the following two questions:

   a) Could we argue that metalinguistic reflection is not exclusively a function of output? Could learners engage in metalinguistic reflection during interpretive communication activities?

   b) If we agree that acquisition is a (mostly) implicit process, what role could metalinguistic reflection, if any, play in facilitating language development?

3) Think about all the different ways we communicate in writing: social media posts, reviews, personal profiles, emails, shopping lists, greeting cards, etc. How do they compare with what your students write in class, or what you have written in language classes as a student?

4) According to ACTFL (2012a) Proficiency Guidelines novice learners can write lists, sentence fragments, and formulaic expressions. Yet, in many introductory-level courses, students are typically asked to write short paragraphs that not only consist of complete sentences, but also reflect some type of cohesive organization. Instructors justify this approach by saying that students should be able to transfer their writing skills from their native language(s) (i.e., if they can write cohesive paragraphs in one language, they should be able to do the same in any additional languages). What is the problem with this reasoning? And what would you say to a colleague who insists on complete sentences and cohesive paragraphs with novice learners?

5) What role does proficiency level play in how we approach and scaffold the writing process with our students? For instance, would you incorporate peer feedback with novice learners? Would a free-writing activity work with intermediate learners? Do you think advanced learners still need help generating ideas?

6) Is presentational communication always prepared and polished, or could it also be spontaneous? Can you think of examples, where it might be both prepared and also somewhat spontaneous?

7) What similarities and differences are there between presentational speaking and presentational writing? Do you think one is more appropriate for certain proficiency levels than the other? And what about feedback: Do you think teachers approach corrective feedback the same way for both modalities?

8) What are some pros and cons of setting word limits (minimum or maximum) for presentational writing assignments? Does that reflect how we communicate in writing outside of the classroom?

9) We said that presentational communication tends to be polished, but not everyone agrees about what resources students can or should use to polish their language. What are the pros and cons of allowing students to use dictionaries, spell-checking tools, a tutor, or even online translators to complete presentational writing or speaking assignments? If you allow any external resources, how can we help students understand the best ways of using them?

10) Some students tend to have a negative perception of writing assignments. Why do you think some students dread the idea of writing a paper? And what can we teachers do to foment a more positive perception of writing? Reflect on the characteristics of writing prompts, as well as how we respond to what learners write.

11) In Chapter 3, we talked about authentic materials when we discussed different sources of input. Does the distinction between authentic and nonauthentic also apply to output? What audiences would you consider authentic?

12) What are some reasons why teachers feel the need to provide written corrective feedback (i.e., mark or correct errors)? Is there a connection between these reasons and what we previously discussed regarding teachers' views on the need to provide explicit grammar instruction or explanations?

13) Imagine that the following feedback was given to a student in a first-year Spanish course. The assignment was to write about what they like and dislike about their town. How might the student interpret this feedback? And what could have been more useful feedback in terms of language development?

> *This is very interesting, but be careful with gender agreement and verb conjugations. And next time, use more words from the chapter vocab list.*

Observation and Application Activities

1) Ask a language educator to share with you a writing assignment from one of the courses they teach, or look at the writing section of a language textbook, and then write some notes on the following:

   a) Would you say that, overall, the emphasis is on the process or the product?

   b) Are the purpose of the writing and the role of the audience clear, or does it seem like students are submitting their work mainly to be graded?

   c) What strategies are used to help students generate and organize their ideas?

   d) What strategies are used to help students revise their writing?

   e) Are the expectations of text type, function, and accuracy realistic and in line with the learners' proficiency level?

   Considering all your observations, are there any aspects of the assignment you would expand or modify? If so, how?

2) Interview a few language educators about their views on written corrective feedback. If possible, try to ask instructors of different languages and levels. Once you have collected several responses, analyze them in terms of what we discussed in this chapter. Here are some questions to consider:

   a) How do they view corrective feedback overall: positively (useful) or negatively (detrimental)?

   b) Do their practices or views change depending on the level of the course they teach?

   c) If they provide corrective feedback on form, how do they decide what to focus on? And what do students do with their feedback?

   d) If they don't provide corrective feedback on form, is that decision based mainly on pedagogical or practical factors?

   e) In what ways do they help learners revise their writing? For example, do learners engage in peer feedback sessions? Are they allowed to use online tools or outside help for editing?

3) Below is a writing prompt for intermediate-low learners. What type of scaffolding would you do to turn it into a guided presentational writing task? Write all the steps involved, as if it were one of the examples we provided in this chapter. Feel free to modify any parts of the prompt as you see fit. And don't forget to include the audience's role: What will others do with this information?

   A group of exchange students is coming to your school. They want to know what your town looks like and what activities people do in their spare time. Provide lots of details!

Chapter 6
Interaction

Pre-test

Before reading this chapter, indicate whether the following statements are true or false, based on what you know or believe . . . for now!

- Interaction entails the spontaneous, synchronous, and purposeful exchange of meaning.
- Negotiation of meaning during interaction contributes to language development.
- Recasts are the most effective way of providing oral corrective feedback.
- The teacher shouldn't be the only person students interact with: Peer interaction has its merits too.
- Decision-making tasks tend to be more appropriate for novice learners, whereas information-gap tasks require a higher proficiency level.

Once you have finished, or while you are reading this chapter, verify your answers

WHAT DO I NEED TO KNOW?

Characteristics of Interpersonal Communication

We saved the best, or the hardest, for last! Interacting with another person usually requires both understanding and producing meaning in real time. That's quite a workout for the brain! Of course, interpersonal communication or interaction doesn't have to be synchronous (in real time). Haven't you ever engaged in a long back-and-forth discussion over email, or social media? In this chapter, though, we will focus on oral, synchronous interaction, since having a conversation is what most people want to do when learning another language.

Let's start by reviewing the key characteristics of interpersonal communication:

- An information gap between interlocutors (i.e., one person doesn't know what the other one will say)
- A purposeful back-and-forth exchange where participants are actively invested in understanding and expressing meaning (i.e., not just practicing or merely commenting on what someone said/ wrote)

So, for instance, if you ask students to take turns reading a dialogue from their textbook, that doesn't count because it can be done without the students understanding a single word. What if students write out a dialogue first, and then they act it out in front of the class? That wouldn't count as interaction or interpersonal communication either since it lacks an information gap between interlocutors. In other words, one person knows exactly what the other one will say, and thus, there is no true "back and forth." The part where students are working together to write the dialogue could potentially count, but it depends a lot on how it is carried out. The part about acting out the dialogue itself is definitely not interpersonal communication.

While it is true that having learners act out a script does not count as interaction, that doesn't mean that the only way to do interpersonal communication is to ask learners to have a spontaneous conversation (i.e., here's the topic—ready, set, go!). As we discussed in Chapter 1, spontaneity is not the *sine qua non* of interpersonal communication. Scaffolding and preparation could, in fact, be necessary for successful interaction. This is especially true for novice learners, who cannot have a conversation 100% on their own, on the spot, and without much preparation or structure. It is also applicable to intermediate, and even some advanced, learners; for instance, students could prepare some questions before video chatting with speakers of the target language, and it would certainly still count as interpersonal communication.

And even though we will be focusing on synchronous interaction, it's worth clarifying a gray area when it comes to asynchronous communication. For example, if I write a forum post about my hobbies, and someone responds indicating whether they also like any of the hobbies I mentioned, is that interpersonal? Our stance is that if there is no "back and forth," it is not interpersonal, but rather presentational with audience participation. As we saw in Chapter 5, having the audience do something with the information conveyed is a key aspect of a good presentational task. Now that we're on the same page about what we mean by "interaction," let's delve into its role in language development.

The Interaction Hypothesis

According to Long (1996), interaction facilitates language development "because it connects input, internal learner capacities, particularly selective attention, and output in productive ways" (pp. 451–52). During interaction, learners may realize what they do not know how to say or notice a mismatch between their utterance and the target language. Both cognitive processes are thought to sensitize learners to the occurrence of those particular forms in future input, thus increasing the likelihood of making form-meaning connections.

The Interaction Hypothesis, like the Output Hypothesis, stems from the premise that input is necessary but insufficient. Both hypotheses view focusing the learners' attention on form in a communication-oriented environment to facilitate language development. However, while the Output Hypothesis does not consider the benefits of output to be dependent upon immediate interactional feedback, the Interaction Hypothesis is quite specific about the importance of negotiation episodes between interlocutors. What do they negotiate? They engage in negotiation of form and meaning triggered by an effort to communicate (i.e., to understand the interlocutor or to express meaning). Not everyone agrees about the role of conscious attention to form in language development; however, the Interaction Hypothesis does view negotiation of form and meaning as essential, so let's discuss it in greater length.

Negotiation of Form and Meaning

The term "form-focused episode" refers to any point in the interaction where interlocutors focus on language itself: They might need help with how to say something, they might be unsure about the appropriateness of what they are saying, or they might notice something that isn't quite right about what someone else said . . . and feel the need to point it out! Although the examples we provide below involve a teacher and a student, form-focused episodes occur in all interaction types, including when learners interact with each other.

Form-focused episodes can be preemptive or reactive. A preemptive form-focused episode occurs in anticipation of a potential problem; for instance, teachers can typically anticipate which forms or words might be tricky for students, and so they address them before the issue even arises. Here's an example of preemptive focus on form, where the teacher anticipates a lack of understanding of the word "magazines," even though that may or may not be the case:

> Teacher: Do you prefer reading newspapers or magazines? Magazines are publications like *Vogue*, *Cosmo*, and *People*. Those are magazines.
>
> Student: I prefer magazines.

In this other example, the teacher preemptively turns the learner's attention to the irregular form of the verb "bought," anticipating that the learner may say something like "buyed":

Teacher: What did she buy? She bought . . . Remember that "bought" is the past tense of "buy." It's irregular.

Student: She bought a book.

Reactive form-focused episodes are exchanges involving corrective feedback, given that they occur in reaction to a non-target-like form. Here's an example of an exchange illustrating a reactive form-focused episode:

Teacher: What are you doing this weekend?

Student: Go pool.

Teacher: Are you going to play pool, like billiards? (*mimics the motion of playing pool*) Or are you going to a pool, to swim? (*mimics the motion of swimming*)

Student: To swim. Yes.

Teacher: Oh, I see! That sounds fun!

The example above involves a specific type of corrective feedback called a "clarification request." Other common types of feedback are: recasts, elicitation, and explicit metalinguistic correction (i.e., the teacher provides a brief explanation of what needs to be changed and why). A recast is a partial or total reformulation of the utterance, aiming to provide the correct form without disrupting the flow of communication. It is considered an input-providing form of feedback. Elicitation, on the other hand, is output-prompting because it is intended to push the learner to provide the correct form in response to rising intonation or other verbal cues. To put it simply, the main differences between recasts and elicitation are as follows:

	Does the teacher provide the correct form?	Is the learner required to self-correct?
Recast	Yes	No
Elicitation (a.k.a. prompt)	No	Yes

Here's an example of a recast, where the teacher reformulates and keeps the conversation going:

Teacher: What did you do last weekend?

Student: My brother come home.

Teacher: Oh, your brother came home! And what did you do with him?

Student: We went shopping.

And here's an example of elicitation, where the teacher questions the learner's word choice and prompts them to modify their utterance:

Teacher: What are you doing after school?

Student: Go home, make homework.

Teacher: Make your homework? Make?

Student: Do! Do homework, yes.

Teacher: Ah, OK.

One of the reasons why recasts tend to be viewed favorably by language educators is that they are relatively unobtrusive: A teacher can provide a correction without shifting the focus of the conversation too far from meaning. With elicitation, on the other hand, the correction is more obvious and less natural: Who would respond like that, other than a language teacher?

At the same time, the relatively implicit nature of recasts can also be considered a drawback: The learner might not even notice a difference between their own utterance and the teacher's. In some cases, the recast may lead to confusion if a student misunderstands the teacher's intentions, as in the example below.

Teacher: What are you doing this weekend?

Student: I go swim.

Teacher: I'm going to swim.

Student: You go swim, too?

The degree of explicitness of recasts varies widely. For instance, a recast can be made more explicit by emphasizing or repeating the reformulated portion. Among teachers, it is quite common to hear that they only use recasts because they don't want to interrupt the flow of communication, but as we can see in the example above, recasts can sometimes end up sounding just as unnatural and intrusive as a prompt might be.

In case you're wondering . . .

Does the proficiency level of the learners affect the effectiveness of recasts versus prompts? What research tells us is that proficiency may affect whether learners notice recasts as corrections (Philp, 2003): The higher the proficiency, the better able learners are to realize that something was corrected. This finding makes sense, but it would be dangerous to conclude that recasts are not effective with novice learners or that novice learners need more explicit corrections. If there is anything novice learners need it is more input, which is precisely what recasts provide.

Researchers classify and sub-categorize feedback moves differently, and as important as that is for research purposes, educators rarely have consistent control of the type of feedback they provide in the classroom. In fact, teachers typically combine several different types of feedback within the same exchanges, which is not a bad thing. If you were hoping for us to tell you what the best feedback strategy is, we're sorry to disappoint you. The truth is that "there is no corrective feedback recipe" (Ellis, 2008, p. 106). Our general advice would be to choose the least intrusive way of providing feedback, giving priority to comprehensibility over accuracy, especially with novice learners.

The Role of Interactional Feedback

In Chapter 5, we talked about feedback on written production, and we cast some doubts regarding its effectiveness. All of the caveats and potential roles of feedback we mentioned still apply here. Let's review the main points, particularly those that are most relevant for feedback that occurs within oral interaction.

First and foremost, we cannot expect feedback to have a direct or immediate effect on students' language development. Even if you clearly signal that something wasn't right, and they notice the issue and even produce the correct form right in front of you, don't be surprised if they later produce the same non-target-like form again. And again. And a few more times after that, which is an understandable source of frustration for teachers. Perhaps the most effective way of curbing that frustration is to go back to basics and reflect on why it happens. Although it sounds straightforward to say that feedback helps learners confirm or reject interlanguage hypotheses (i.e., they try something out and see how well-received it is by their interlocutor), acquisition is an internal process that we can't consciously control.

Does this mean that we should not provide any type of feedback ever? No. First, depending on the type of feedback, it *might* help provide additional input that *may* contribute to developing the students' linguistic systems. Second, we are not saying that feedback has absolutely no effect at all, not even on explicit knowledge. In fact, the consensus appears to be that corrective feedback contributes to explicit knowledge, and learners use *some* explicit knowledge in monitored production (e.g., writing).

So, what do we do? Here are, once again, the implications for the classroom, as best as we can summarize them:

- **Curb your expectations:** Providing learners with feedback on form within meaningful interaction *might* help *some* learners (or maybe just one!) make the right form-meaning connections, but you are bound to be disappointed if you expect corrective feedback to result in error-free output.

- **Don't ignore the affective side of feedback:** Frequent error correction might a have negative impact on your students' confidence and motivation. This outcome is partly why Dörnyei (1994) suggested to "use motivating feedback by making your feedback informational rather than controlling; giving positive competence feedback, pointing out the value of accomplishment; and not over-reacting to errors" (p. 282).

- **Let it go, let it go:** There is nothing wrong with letting some or most errors go. Lack of correction does not lead students to automatically conclude that whatever they said was the "correct" form and that they will now say it that way forever and ever. Their language is a constant work in progress, and students themselves are the first ones to tell you that.

In case you're wondering . . .

Doesn't research show that explicit feedback is better? Just as with grammar instruction, research once again claims that explicit is better. Coincidence? We think not. As you might recall from Chapter 3, the question is: better for what? We can't take research findings out of context and make blanket statements about "benefits." Explicit feedback may indeed help learners gain explicit knowledge about the language, so when they do an activity where they can monitor their production carefully, which is often the case in research studies, the results reveal "benefits" in favor of explicit feedback. Plus, some participants quickly figure out what target structure the researcher is really interested in, so they are extra careful about using it correctly.

Interlocutor Characteristics

Most of the initial research on the Interaction Hypothesis focused on teacher-student interaction. However, we know that students often engage in pair or group work that requires them to interact with other learners, and it is important to understand the merits and shortcomings of different interaction types, particularly so we don't rush to erroneous conclusions like "the only source of input should be the teacher" or "learner interaction is detrimental to their language development."

Research has revealed some advantages and disadvantages of learner-learner interaction when compared to instructor-led class discussions (Sato & Lyster, 2007; Zhao & Bitchener, 2007). Some of the advantages appear to be:

- More opportunities for negotiation of meaning and form when interacting with peers

- More willingness to ask questions about language and seek help from peers as opposed to the instructor
- Higher occurrence of modified output (i.e., they produced the "revised" version of what they had said) following feedback from peers

Among potential drawbacks of learner-learner interaction, the two most obvious are:

- Inconsistent and sometimes inaccurate feedback, although the incidence of incorrect feedback is overall relatively low
- Inability to resolve some queries (i.e., when they ask their peers for help, they might not be able to provide an answer)

That being said, establishing a clear comparison between learner-learner and teacher-learner interaction may not be entirely feasible or even desirable, simply because the two are very different in nature. Furthermore, any advantages and drawbacks of peer interaction are dependent upon a myriad of factors, including: proficiency level, task type, attitude toward the tasks, peer- and self-perceptions, etc. All these factors can also play a role when it comes to grouping strategies. As Storch and Aldosari (2013) point out, "when pairing students, it is not only proficiency difference which needs to be taken into consideration, but also the kind of relationship learners form when working in pairs" (p. 46). Therefore, giving advice on best practices for grouping learners is more complicated than it seems. The most important suggestion we can give you is: Get to know your students so that you can try to pair them up based not only on their language level, but also on their personality and preferences.

In case you're wondering . . .

Do students learn the wrong forms when they interact with each other? First of all, research has consistently shown that in the overwhelming majority of negotiation episodes, learners can and do provide each other with target-like resolutions. Inevitably, in a few cases, learners reach the wrong resolutions, and some studies have documented that learners retain some of that information (Adams, 2007; Zhao & Bitchener, 2007) Nevertheless, this disadvantage of learner-learner interaction does not diminish its positive effects, and we also need to keep in mind that just because there was uptake or retention of information in posttests, that doesn't mean learners are now "stuck" producing those forms forever. Plus, the underlying assumption of questioning the value of peer interaction based on students learning each other's "errors" seems to be that the teacher is never the source of non-target-like information. Is that always the case? Something to think about!

Scaffolding Interaction

Some teachers are hesitant about incorporating learner-learner interaction at the novice level mainly because they worry that students will not use the target language or they will get off task. Many times, though not always, those issues are in part due to what we are asking learners to do. Let's dissect this example from a first-year course where learners are novice-mid/high:

> Students work in pairs: They need to ask each other questions about family traditions and celebrations, and they need to ask follow-up questions on the information their partner is sharing. For example: "What do you eat that day?"

The two main issues with an activity like that are:

- It seems to lack a purpose or goal. What will the other student do with the information their partner is sharing? When we ask learners to do something without a concrete purpose, we are increasing the odds they won't stay on task.
- It seems to assume that learners can keep the conversation going on their own, but novice learners are almost exclusively reactive. Even though they might be able to ask a few formulaic questions (e.g., "Why?"), their partner might not be able to provide a response. When we ask learners to do something above their level, we are increasing the odds that they will use the shared language more than the target language.

When creating interpersonal tasks, it is not enough to put ourselves in the students' shoes, but rather to keep in mind what learners can do at their level. As educators, we are quite talented at thinking of questions to keep a conversation going (and we forget how hard that can be!). We also know what types of questions are too difficult and need to be rephrased or avoided when interacting with a novice-level speaker, but we can't expect learners to have the same skills we do.

How can we properly scaffold an activity like that? First, we need to start with a goal; for instance: to determine similarities and differences between the way we celebrate our favorite holidays. Then, learners could create a mind map or graphic organizer where they brainstorm words or phrases related to various aspects of their favorite holiday; the teacher would provide the categories they should focus on: food, drinks, activities, people, clothing, weather, etc. Then, learners could come up with yes/no questions based on the information in their graphic organizers (e.g., "Do you celebrate with your family?", "Do you eat turkey?", etc.). As learners interview each other, they could take notes in the form of Venn diagrams (i.e., what they have in common and what's unique to each of them). Using that information, they can summarize the similarities and differences between their own and their partner's favorite holiday. The teacher should provide some sentence starters and examples to help learners get their thoughts organized into a few sentences. As learners present their conclusions, the teacher could keep track of responses on the board and then guide students to notice patterns among all of the responses in the class.

In case you're wondering . . .

How do I get students to interact more spontaneously? Although you might be tempted to think that unstructured tasks will lead to more spontaneous language use, it is important to create well-structured interpersonal activities that are appropriate for the learners' proficiency level so they don't become frustrated (e.g., when they don't even know where to start) or uninterested (e.g., when the purpose is unclear). The type of output we expect should also be in line with their proficiency level. It's OK for novice learners to respond with isolated words! Learners will say more as they acquire the language and develop communicative ability thanks to the opportunities we provide for them to engage in communication. Of course, depending on the task, it may be beneficial for learners to be gently pushed to expand on their ideas (e.g., "Can you tell me a little more?").

Characteristics of Tasks

A pedagogical approach embraced by supporters of the Interaction Hypothesis is Task-based Language Teaching (TBLT), where lessons or units are organized around tasks, as opposed to texts or grammar structures. What is a task? It depends on who you ask! (Yes—We're poets and we know it!) We won't bog you down with the million and one definitions of "task" here. We will stay true to form and give you the concise version of the common ground among them.

A task, by itself, is "the hundred and one things people do in everyday life, at work, at play, and in between. 'Tasks' are the things people will tell you they do if you ask them and they are not applied linguists" (Long, 1985, p. 89). For example, tasks include: following directions, deciding what movie to watch, planning a trip or a party, asking for restaurant recommendations, teaching someone how to cook a dish or play a game, responding to an email, etc.

Thus, a pedagogic task (i.e., what you do in the classroom) within TBLT is all about language use involving communicative functions that happen outside of the classroom: asking for information, explaining or describing something, consulting with someone to make a decision, etc. However, they don't necessarily have to be identical to "real-life" situations. Ellis et al. (2019) make it a point to clarify that tasks involve "language use that is interactionally rather than situationally authentic" (p. 342). For example, if one student describes a picture for another student to draw, that would be interactionally authentic because providing detailed information about what something looks like is indeed a communicative function, but it would lack situational authenticity since we don't normally ask people to describe things so we can draw them.

Furthermore, the pedagogic tasks you use should be relatable and relevant to your learners, as opposed to just any task anyone does in "real life." For instance, interviewing someone for a job is probably not something that most high school or even college students do. Now, if you taught a group of managers at an international company, then that might very well be a suitable task to build a lesson or unit around.

Even if you don't plan on adopting TBLT as your approach, understanding and applying the criteria for what constitutes a task can be very useful as you create activities, particularly those targeting the interpersonal mode.

In case you're wondering . . .

Do all tasks require learners to be interacting with each other? No, they don't! There are indeed input-providing tasks. In fact, we already mentioned one in Chapter 1: Students read a series of classified ads of houses and apartments for rent; the teacher describes their own housing preferences, and students select one of the places described in the classified ads that they think would be the best option for their instructor. Another example of an input-providing task would be: The teacher gives directions; students have to draw the route on a map and then indicate where they ended up.

Ellis (2009) outlines the following minimum criteria to create tasks:

- Learners should be engaged in understanding and expressing meaning, as opposed to practicing a specific form or set of vocab.
- There should be a "gap"; in other words, the information conveyed should be unknown to the other interlocutor(s). Essentially, if all interlocutors know what the other person is going to say, then there is no "gap."
- Learners choose the linguistic and nonlinguistic resources needed to complete the task. That doesn't mean it's a completely unstructured activity. Some tasks naturally prompt the use of certain words and certain structures, and all tasks have instructions. This criterion simply refers to not forcing students to interact in a certain way (e.g., "use complete sentences," "be sure to use irregular verbs," etc.).
- There is a concrete, nonlinguistic outcome. In other words, learners should know what they are trying to accomplish by exchanging information, and at the end of the task, we should be able to tell whether they accomplished it.

Let's take a look at two examples: The first one fulfills all four criteria, but the second one does not. Notice that, in both cases, criterion #1 is met: Learners are expressing and understanding meaning. However, that is not enough.

> **Example A:** Students work in pairs. The teacher gives one of the learners a picture of a house. One student describes the picture for the other one to draw it as closely to the original as possible but without being able to see it.

- There is a gap: One learner knows something the other doesn't know but needs to know.
- Learners choose the resources needed to complete the task: Their interaction is not restricted or controlled.
- The goal is not related to language, but rather to draw the picture as closely to the original as possible, and we can indeed determine if that goal was accomplished or not at the end of the task.

> **Example B:** The teacher displays a picture of a house; students work in pairs. They take turns asking questions about the picture to their classmate (e.g., "What color is the roof? How many windows are there?"). Each student has to ask five questions using at least three different question words (where, how many, what, etc.).

- There is no gap: everyone sees the picture, so everyone has all the same information.
- Learners are not choosing the resources needed to complete the task: They have to ask a specific number of questions worded in a specific way (whether they want to or not!).
- There isn't a concrete, nonlinguistic purpose to this activity: The goal is entirely related to language (most likely, asking questions).

If you are having *déjà vu* and wondering where you heard this all before, it's because we have been making these points all along. In Chapter 1, we said that activities should involve the purposeful interpretation and/or expression of meaning, which implies having clear answers for both of these questions: (1) What information or content is being conveyed? and (2) What will others do with the information? Example B doesn't have an answer for the second question. Then, in Chapter 3, we said that learners should be able and compelled to understand language. If we were learners participating in the activity described in Example B, the only thing we would be compelled to do is ask: "Why are you asking me these questions? Can't you see the picture?"

Now, let's look at a different example, which may look like a task but actually fails to meet the criteria.

> **Example C:** Student A has the steps to prepare a dish. Student B has the list of ingredients. Students are told to work together to give each other the information they need to have a complete recipe.

There is indeed a gap, but the goal of having a complete recipe could be accomplished without paying attention to meaning: One student could just read the list of ingredients, and the other one could write them down without understanding what those ingredients are. Furthermore, students are not choosing the resources needed to accomplish the task. Dictation is not interpersonal communication!

In case you're wondering . . .

Are these tasks the same thing that VanPatten (2017) talks about when he says that they should be the backbone of our units? As we said in Chapter 1, Van-Patten (2017) underscores the need to respect the context of the classroom, where learners are not tourists, salesclerks, or anything like that. TBLT is not as restrictive when it comes to the context, and oftentimes, students are put in situations that resemble life outside of the classroom. What both perspectives have in common is that tasks involve a communicative exchange because it is focused on meaning, and learners need to understand each other to accomplish a nonlinguistic goal. And we fully agree with both camps in that meaningful, purposeful communication should be at the core of every lesson.

Types of Tasks

Now that we know the basic criteria for tasks, let's talk about two of the most common types of tasks. There are more, and they can be classified in other ways (e.g., focused versus unfocused), but in case you haven't noticed, we're all about simplifying and being concise.

- **Information-gap tasks** (a.k.a., "info-gap tasks"), where learners exchange specific information that the other person needs in order to complete the task. They can be one-way (i.e., one learner holds all the info that the other needs), or two-way (i.e., they each have some info that their interlocutor needs). Example A above is a one-way, info-gap task.

- **Decision-making tasks,** where learners come to a consensus regarding a particular situation. The classic example is planning a party for a limited number of guests and on a budget. Students make decisions based on their preferences and viewpoints, which they need to convey to each other (thus, constituting a "gap"!).

Each type has its pros and cons. Info-gap tasks can be good for learners who need more structure, and they also allow the instructor to have more control over the content that students will be exchanging. On the other hand, some learners might find info-gap tasks to be too contrived or inauthentic. Some students might think that a two-way, spot-the-differences task is fun and really get into it, whereas others might do the bare minimum to get it over with. Decision-making tasks can spark creativity in students and let them take more ownership of their learning, depending on what they need to decide. At the same time, it is more difficult for lower-level students to carry out a decision-making task: They might avoid disagreeing or negotiating with their interlocutors simply because they don't have the necessary skills to do so. Agreeing with everything someone else says, regardless of how you truly feel, is certainly much easier.

As you will see in the examples in the next section, activities can foster interpersonal communication without necessarily being info-gap or decision-making tasks. Knowing about different types of tasks is simply a way of expanding your teaching repertoire. Not everything needs to be a task! As long as learners are engaged in purposeful interpretation and expression of meaning, you're on the right track toward helping them develop communicative ability in the target language.

In a nutshell

Before we move on to classroom examples, summarize five main points from this chapter. What are your own takeaways?

_____

_____

_____

_____

_____

Would you like to learn more?
Go to **www.hackettpublishing.com/common-ground-resources**
for a list of suggested readings, webinars, and other resources.

What Does It Look Like in the Classroom?

Example 1: Menus (Info-Gap Task)

This example consists of a two-way, spot-the-differences task; in other words, each student has some of the information, and they need to interact to accomplish the objective of spotting the differences between two menus. This way, the instructor can incorporate culturally relevant information. Furthermore, unlike other spot-the-differences tasks, where the goal might seem a bit artificial (i.e., just finding random differences), the task of comparing two restaurants has interactional authenticity, and it can be expanded into a decision-making task.

Proficiency level: Novice-high

Step 1: In preparation for the task, the instructor creates or adapts two restaurant menus from a country where the target language is spoken. Some items are identical, and others are different. Here are some examples of potential similarities and differences:

- Both restaurants have the exact same three entrées, but one of them has a fourth entrée.
- Both serve ice cream, but they have different flavors available.
- Both restaurants serve the exact same dish, but the price is different.

Step 2: Each student sees only one of the menus. They work together to find as many differences as possible between the two. As they spot a difference, they write it down to keep track of it. The teacher can provide a list of useful phrases and remind them to inquire about all aspects of the menu (i.e., items, prices, dish descriptions, etc.), but students should not be obligated to interact in a specific way. Below is an example of what the interaction may look like:

Student A: My restaurant has three appetizers. You?

Student B: No, two.

Student A: Oh! A difference!

Students write down "2 vs. 3 appetizers" in their list of differences.

Student B: What appetizers in yours?

Student A: Spinach dip.

Student B: Yes.

Student A: Chips and salsa.

Student B: No. I have chips and guacamole.

Student A: Another difference!

Students write down "salsa vs. guacamole" in their list of differences.

Student B: How much is spinach dip?

Student A: $10.

Student B: Only $5 here.

Student A: Cheap!

Student B: Yes. Your restaurant is expensive!

Students write down "$5 vs. $10 for spinach dip" in their list of differences.

The interaction continues until students think they have found all the differences or until time is up.

Step 3: The teacher asks pairs to share what differences they found. Other groups can add to their lists any differences they may have missed.

Step 4 (optional): Based on how the two restaurants compare, students decide which one they would choose to go to dinner. They can also briefly state why by referring to the comparisons they wrote down in Step 2.

Example 2: Shopping (Info-Gap Task)

In this task, one student is assigned the role of customer and the other is the salesperson. Before students interact, there is some preparation that makes each exchange unique to each pair of learners. Alternatively, the task can also be done with information the teacher provides. Notice that each student receives a different set of instructions, and they should not have access to each other's materials. Specific details within this example can be adapted, as needed, depending on the language you teach. Other details (e.g., the budget, the available items, the number of days, etc.) can also be adapted, depending on how much of a challenge students should work around.

Proficiency level: Novice-high/intermediate-low

Step 1: Before students interact, everyone should understand their role and context.

- **Student A:** You are traveling to (*city where the target language is spoken*), but your luggage is delayed. The airline has given you $40 to buy what you need for the next two days until your luggage arrives. First, make a list of all the toiletries and clothes you will need to buy. Put an asterisk next to the items you think are crucial. You may or may not be able to buy everything on your list, so you may need to prioritize!

- **Student B:** You are the salesperson. Here's a list of items that you have in your store (*teacher provides the list*). First, look up information online to determine the prices of each of these items (*teacher provides links to a couple of department stores in that city*). Write the prices next to each one.

Step 2: Once students have their lists ready, they can interact. Student A should keep track of how much they are spending so they don't go over budget. The teacher can provide a list of useful phrases ("how much is it?"), but students should choose the linguistic resources needed to accomplish the task (i.e., they should not be obligated to interact in a specific way). This is what the interaction may look like:

Student A: I need toothbrush. Do you have toothbrush?

Student B: Yes, many toothbrush. What color?

Student A: I don't know. Red?

Student B: OK.

Student A: How much?

Student B: Red is $5. White is $2.

Student A: OK, white. Thank you.

Student B: You need toothpaste?

Student A: Yes! How much?

Student B: $4.

Student A: OK. I need pajamas also.

Student B: What size?

Student A: Big.

Student B: Large?

Student A: Yes.

Student B: $35.

Student A: Very expensive! No money. No cheaper?

Student B: No, sorry. It's very good pajama.

Student A: OK, no pajama. I sleep with T-shirt.

Student B: Haha! OK.

Student A: Also . . . comb. For hair. You have comb?

Student B: I don't have comb.

Student A: Oh no!

Student B: Sorry.

The interaction continues until Student A has bought everything on their list or reached their budget limit.

Step 3: After the interaction concludes, students will share with the class what items they were able to buy and which ones they were not (if any). The teacher keeps track of the items that most travelers bought and leads a brief discussion on essential items. The teacher can also discuss differences in prices or item availability between countries.

Example 3: Planning an Itinerary (Decision-Making Task)

This example describes a decision-making task, where students must work together to come up with one concrete plan according to certain requirements and restrictions. In this scenario, students are planning a weekend excursion with a group of students who are visiting from another school. Other alternatives for similar decision-making tasks could include planning a party, organizing a fundraiser, deciding what show or movie to watch, etc.

Proficiency level: Intermediate-low

Step 1: The teacher explains the context of the task and what goal students need to accomplish:

A group of students from ABC School will be visiting our school next month. In your groups, plan an itinerary for them. Your itinerary should include:

- Two class visits
- One event organized by the school
- One full-day excursion outside of the school
- Lunch and dinner at different restaurants

Keep in mind the following information:

- Some of the students are afraid of heights.
- Some of the students are vegetarian.
- The teachers would like students to experience a variety of activities (sports, arts, science, etc.).

Step 2: Each student works individually to brainstorm ideas for the itinerary. They can also look up information online about restaurants and attractions where they live, and they can consult their school's calendar to find the school-related event.

Step 3: In their small groups, students share their ideas with each other and come to a consensus. All members of the group need to agree about their final choices for the itinerary.

Step 4: Each group presents their ideas to the rest of the class. They need to provide convincing arguments in favor of the choices they made. The class votes for the best choices overall and finalizes the plans for the itinerary. The teacher can facilitate the voting and the discussion by asking students to list pros and cons in case of disagreements.

Example 4: Mystery Interviewee

Students interview each other as if they were one of the characters in one of the stories they read in the course or movie/video they watched, or any other person students learned about (e.g., a historical figure, an influential person, a celebrity, etc.). The teacher can provide a list of possibilities. First, the teacher acts as the mystery interviewee to model the activity: Students ask questions, and the teacher responds as that character/person, and the students guess. Then, the students interview each other.

Proficiency level: Intermediate-low/mid

Step 1: The teacher gives a quick overview of the activity. Students prepare questions that would help them figure out who the mystery interviewee is. The teacher can help them with some ideas, such as:

- What are your favorite foods?
- What is your family like?
- Where do you live?

Step 2: Students interview the teacher (who has secretly chosen a new "identity"). Students guess who it is, and the teacher confirms.

Step 3: Students select a character/person for themselves, and they review information or do additional research so they can be prepared to answer questions as if they were that character or person. They can use the questions they came up with in Step 1 as a guide, but they should not write anything down.

Step 4: Students interview each other. If they don't know specific information being asked about the person, they should still answer, even if it is just a guess. The interviewer should take notes or record the interview.

Step 5: Once all interviews have been conducted, the interviewers reveal who they think they interviewed, and the other student will confirm.

Step 6 (optional): Students create a final product consisting of an interview for a magazine, titled "Exclusive Interview with _____." If needed, any details or information provided by the other student in Step 4 can be revised or expanded.

Example 5: Visual Analysis through Picture Talk

This is an example of student-teacher interaction where the discussion happens with the entire class. Unlike more traditional "picture talk," where the main reason for the teacher to ask questions is language practice (i.e., there is no greater goal other than to interact), the purpose for the questions is to analyze a painting. Visual analysis is a great way not only to engage students in meaningful communication, but also to help them think critically about what they see (i.e., go beyond superficial descriptions), which is a transferable skill. For this type of activity to be successful, the choice of artwork is key: A painting with multiple elements and a clear message works best. As students become more comfortable with visual analysis, two paintings could be selected for a comparative analysis. This activity could also be adapted for more advanced students by putting them in charge of leading the discussion after the teacher has modeled it.

Proficiency level: Intermediate-low

Step 1: The teacher displays the painting of a mural. Students are given one minute to observe it in silence. Then, they individually write a list of things they see in it. If they don't know the words in the target language, they can write it in the shared language.

Step 2: Students share with the class the words they wrote, and the teacher writes them on the board, providing the translation in the target language, if needed. This list can serve as a vocabulary reference throughout the conversation.

Step 3: The teacher asks students a series of questions in the target language about the painting, carefully guiding them to discover the underlying message of the artwork. If the need for new words arises during the discussion, the teacher adds them to the list of words on the board. Some of the questions the teacher asks are:

- What do you see first? What does it look like? What adjectives can we use to describe it?
- What do we associate with that object? Is it something positive or negative?

- What is the position of the figures? Are they looking at one thing or are they looking in different directions?
- What colors do you notice? Are they bright or not? What emotions do you associate with those colors?
- How are the different objects arranged? Does it look crowded, or is there a lot of empty space?
- What contrasts do you notice? What patterns or similarities do you notice?

Step 4: After the discussion, students individually write down the ideas that were mentioned, summarizing the visual analysis. They can jot down ideas in a graphic organizer, like this one:

	What I notice	What I think it suggests
Colors		
Objects		
Lines, texture		
Composition		

Step 5 (optional): Each student chooses a new painting, out of a series of choices provided by the teacher, and they write a few sentences comparing the painting analyzed by the whole class and the new painting they selected. The teacher should provide sentence starters and connectors as scaffolding.

Example 6: Simulated Interview

In this example, the instructor interviews each student as potential candidates for a variety of volunteering opportunities, thus providing a clear, nonlinguistic (and non-pedagogic) goal to the exchange. The possible volunteering opportunities can be existing positions in the community that the teacher can look up ahead of time, or they can be generic in nature (e.g., tutoring at a school, preparing food at the soup kitchen, helping at an animal shelter, etc.). Instructor-led individual interviews can serve as a form of assessment or in preparation for a performance assessment; it would most likely occur at the end of the course or unit. By having the instructor conduct the interview, the level of the questions can be adjusted to each student's performance.

Proficiency level: Intermediate-mid

Step 1: The instructor provides an overview of the task to the student, explaining the objective and the structure of the interview.

Step 2: The instructor interviews the student. Questions revolve around their studies, interests, hobbies, routines, goals, preferences, and prior experiences. Questions are fairly broad and open so all students have the opportunity to share as much as they want. For example, the teacher might ask:

- Tell me about your studies.
- Why did you decide to study that?
- What types of classes or projects do you enjoy?
- When you are not studying, what do you do?
- Tell me about a typical day (at school/in your job).
- What are your favorite things about what you study/what you do at work?
- What personal qualities describe you? And why?
- Tell me about any work experiences you have had.
- What are some ways you have helped your community?
- What are some social causes that are important to you?

Step 3: At the conclusion of the interview, the instructor makes two recommendations of volunteering opportunities that might be a good fit for the student, who then asks a few questions to decide which one to accept. For instance, interaction may go as follows:

Teacher: Based on what you have shared with me, I have two volunteering opportunities that would be great for you. One of them is a tutoring position at a local school. The other opportunity is at the public library. What questions do you have about these opportunities? What do you want to know?

Student: What is the job at the library?

Teacher: They need volunteers to read books to children on Sundays.

Student: How many hours?

Teacher: You need to be available at least one hour a week.

Students: OK. I like it. I choose the library.

Example 7: Book Club Chat

In this example, student conversations will mimic a book club discussion after reading a novel. It could be done halfway through the book and again at the end. It could also be done after watching a movie as well since the questions would be similar. The key is to focus on the exchange between small groups of students, and the questions should be more about opinions and perspectives, as opposed to mere retrieval of information or facts.

Proficiency level: Intermediate-mid/high

Step 1: The teacher provides some examples of questions such as: Who is your favorite character and why? Do you think this person made a good decision at this point? What do you think will happen in the next chapter?

Step 2: Students brainstorm some follow-up questions from the teacher's questions and some additional questions that would elicit opinions.

Step 3: Students work in small groups and discuss their questions. At the end, they should come up with a list of opinions about the novel that everyone in the group agrees with.

Step 4: Students share their opinions, and the teacher leads the class in co-constructing a collective review based on the opinions from the majority of the students. This approach allows the teacher to provide feedback on form without explicitly correcting students. For example, an exchange between the students and the teacher could look like this:

> Teacher: Let's talk about the main characters. Group 1, what do you think about the characters?
>
> Student: We say they are comics.
>
> Teacher: They're comical, yes!
>
> Student: Yes.
>
> Teacher: I agree. So, let's write: The two main characters are comical. (*Types in the computer, which is hooked up to a projector so everyone can see.*) Great! Group 2, what else can we say about the main characters?

Now That You Know

Discussion and Expansion Questions

1) Research has shown that learners are more prone to focus on form when engaged in tasks that involve writing, as opposed to tasks that are strictly oral (Adams, 2006; Adams & Ross-Feldman, 2008; Cumming, 1990; Williams, 2008), presumably due to the concreteness of the written word, as well as the fact that writing allows for greater processing time than speaking. What are some ways in which you could incorporate a writing component to an interpersonal task?

2) Evaluate these three exchanges. What do you notice with respect to feedback? Could we say that one of these might potentially be more beneficial for language development than the others?

   a) *Student: Me no like spiders.*
      Teacher: I don't like spiders either!

   b) *Student: Me no like spiders.*
      Teacher: Me neither!

   c) *Student: Me no like spiders.*
      Teacher: You don't like them? Me neither!

3) Evaluate this activity, which was marked as "interpersonal communication" in a textbook. Which of the criteria for an interpersonal task are not met? What would you need to modify so it is a task as described in this chapter?

   Ask a classmate about the last time they did the following activities. Write down their answers in complete sentences.
   - *Go to the movies*
   - *Eat at a restaurant*
   - *Swim in the ocean*
   - *Buy something expensive*

4) Out of the four criteria of tasks outlined in this chapter, which one do you think is most often unmet by most activities in language classes? Why do you think it could be particularly challenging for educators to meet that criterion?

5) This activity does not meet the criteria for it to be an info-gap task. Why not?

Instructions for Student A: This is a class schedule of a college student in the United States, but the names of the classes are missing. Your partner has the information you need. Ask your partner questions to complete the schedule.

Mondays & Wednesdays, 9:00 a.m.— _____

Mondays & Wednesdays, 10:00 a.m.— _____

Tuesdays & Thursdays, 1:00 p.m.— _____

Thursdays 3:30 p.m.— _____

Instructions for Student B: This is a class schedule of a college student in the United States. Your partner needs some of the information. Answer their questions to help them complete the schedule.

Mondays & Wednesdays, 9:00 a.m.—Spanish class

Mondays & Wednesdays, 10:00 a.m.—Geography class

Tuesdays & Thursdays, 1:00 p.m.—Chemistry class

Thursdays 3:30 p.m.—Chemistry lab

6) Evaluate the following prompt for an info-gap task: "Work with a partner to find a time to meet to study for an upcoming test." What would the interaction between two students look like? Would you say it is a good info-gap task, or would you change anything?

7) How would you adapt Example 5 (teacher-led visual analysis) if the focus were a song instead of a painting? Write the questions you would ask, and what phrases or sentence starters students could use to discuss various aspects of the song (rhythm, instruments, chorus, etc.). If you have a song in mind that would work for an activity like that, even better!

8) Research on students' and teachers' perceptions and preferences when it comes to feedback tends to indicate that students want to be corrected explicitly, whereas teachers believe implicit feedback is better. What could explain this contrast? And do you think their opinions match the reality of what actually happens in class or what they actually benefit from?

9) Reflect on what the comic strip on the following page says about some teachers' practices when it comes to providing feedback. Do you think it reflects what actually happens in some language classrooms? What would you do differently: provide a recast (i.e. "she *left* you? That's awful!"), or let it go altogether (i.e., "I'm so sorry to hear that")? Would it be the same if it were written corrective feedback?

10) After reading the entire book and reviewing all of the examples, what questions do you have? What are you still grappling with?

Observation and Application Activities

1) Observe an introductory- or intermediate-level class of the language you teach (better, observe one of each level!). Take notes on the following:

   a) Did students engage in any tasks, as defined in this chapter?

   b) What was the ratio of learner-learner versus teacher-learner interaction?

   c) Did you notice any form-focused episodes? Were they reactive or preemptive? Did they focus on vocabulary or grammar?

   d) Did you notice any examples of recasts or prompts? Did the teacher use other ways of providing feedback on form?

2) Interview a few students who are taking language courses to find out their views and preferences about a few things discussed in this chapter. If possible, try to ask students who are at different levels. Here are some questions to consider:

   a) Do they like to be "corrected" when they talk in class? If so, how?

   b) Do they seem to have different preferences when it comes to negotiation of form versus meaning?

   c) How do they feel about the different types of tasks we described in this chapter? Do they do tasks like that in their courses? If so, how engaging do they find them?

    d) What do they think about interacting with other students, versus interacting with their teacher?

3) Create an information-gap task and a decision-making task following the examples we gave in this chapter for one of these topics: travel, weather, school, personal relationships, art and media, sports, cell phones/apps, music, consumerism, or the environment.

Epilogue
Reality Check

Throughout the book, we have discussed some fundamental aspects of second language acquisition and pedagogy, while keeping in mind the reality of the classroom. However, we are very much aware of other constraints that influence pedagogical decisions. In this epilogue, we provide some answers to a few frequently asked "what-ifs" that we typically encounter in our work with language educators who are looking to make changes but feel bound by forces greater than themselves.

Frequently Asked What-Ifs

What if my colleagues seem resistant to changing how they teach or assess students?

The first step is to understand where the resistance comes from. Let's consider a few possible scenarios.

Do they quote research showing that explicit instruction is better? In this case, we gave you enough information in this book to approach the subject. We can't say something is helpful without specifying how that helpfulness was measured. In other words, better for what? And on a related note, it is best to avoid claiming that you follow the ideas or research findings of one scholar in particular. Colleagues who quote research tend to have strong opinions about certain names, and that could muddy the waters unnecessarily. After all, what guides your teaching should be fundamental principles of SLA, rather than famous people in SLA.

Do they say that their students want to learn rules and be corrected? If so, ask them if they are also open to consider other things students want, including just playing video games and making attendance optional. OK, now seriously: Invite your colleagues to reflect on the reason why students say they want rules and error correction. Here's a hint: It has to do with how they have been assessed for years, and not just in language courses. Even if a few students swear they really want to know the rules, chances are that the majority of them want to "have a conversation" or "communicate" in the language. Then, a proficiency-based approach would actually increase learner satisfaction and motivation. If students have never experienced it, though, they have no way of telling you that's what they want. It is certainly a good thing to be aware of students' expectations and preferences, but we should be the ones making pedagogical decisions based on what we know.

Do they claim to teach communicatively (even though their lesson goals revolve around grammar structures to cover), so they don't see what they need to change? If so, then the worst thing you could do is point out that they are wrong not only about what they claim, but also about how they are approaching language instruction. As Fernández (2016) put it, "You do not need enemies if you want change; you need allies" (p. 51). Instead, hear them out and acknowledge the fact that change is not easy, particularly when it involves reconsidering things you held as truths for quite a while, as well as putting a lot of time and creative effort to re-do lessons you thought worked perfectly well. If you used to think the same way they do, admit it and share your own journey. When we feel heard and understood, we are more likely to share what we are grappling with, and that is precisely the start of a fruitful dialogue. Fernández offers other great advice for initiating change, such as being patient and prioritizing improvements.

And speaking of prioritizing, the best place to start is with assessments. As Weir (1990) said, "A test can be a powerful instrument for effective change in the language curriculum" (p. 127). Perhaps your program or department is not quite ready to go with 100% proficiency- or performance-based testing, but it might be open to the idea of including reading or listening components, which will prompt your colleagues to realize that students need help developing their interpretive proficiency . . . and that's quite a battle to win! Slowly but surely, they will start asking themselves key questions such as:

- What linguistic resources do my students *really* need to complete this task?
- Why do they need to know so many words related to one topic?
- Do my students really need to know all the irregular verbs?
- Am I asking students questions because I want to know something about them, or because I want to see if they remember the word for "sister-in-law" or how to say the number "15" in the target language?

Presentational writing is also typically included in most tests, even traditional ones, so now you can focus on making changes to how students are graded, aiming for a rubric like the ones we included in this book, as opposed to taking off points for every error. As a department, you could also grade the presentational writing together using the rubric and discuss what would help students improve their writing.

Another important piece of advice is to make some changes at one level first (e.g., Spanish I), and then work on revamping another level after a year. This approach helps not only to contain unexpected issues within one course, but also to provide a blueprint for other levels to change more efficiently. In other words, the first level to change requires a brave and innovative teacher willing to accept a few bumps on the road, but the process of making changes to other levels goes faster and more smoothly. The key is to make it manageable by starting with a smaller goal and then extending it to include more courses.

What if students don't seem to be making much progress?

Capturing progress when it comes to language development is incredibly challenging. It is slow, variable, and practically intangible. Even if we frame it in terms of communicative ability, we might have different ideas of exactly what counts as "progress."

If you're defining it as moving up the proficiency ladder, keep in mind what we said in Chapter 2: Going from one level to the next takes longer the more advanced your learners are. If your students are starting at novice-low, you will likely see quite a bit of improvement within a year. However, when you reach the intermediate-level range, you might feel as if learners have not made much "progress" in one semester or even one year. Some students may have moved up one sublevel (from low to mid), but don't be surprised if many of them stayed at about the same level. We would argue that instead of concluding that they haven't made progress, you may want to view it this way: Your assessment measure wasn't fine-grained enough to capture the progress they have made.

If your curriculum is organized around performance-based assessments, you are essentially working hard at helping learners develop the skills necessary to perform particular tasks, which are your evidence of progress. In most cases, you can indeed see that students are now better able to perform tasks they couldn't quite do before. Aha! Sweet progress! Of course, there will always be individual differences, so be careful with defining "progress" as a collective phenomenon and avoid comparing students with each other.

Now, if you feel like students are not making progress because they still make a lot of errors when they write or speak, you can probably guess what we are going to respond: Our expectations of accuracy should be in line with our learners' level. The ACTFL Proficiency Guidelines state quite clearly that novice-high writers have "inadequate vocabulary and/or grammar," and even intermediate-high writers could have "numerous and perhaps significant errors" (ACTFL 2012a). The frustration that comes with not seeing improvement in terms of accuracy is usually because we are guilty of rushing a very slow and complex process, as we explained in Chapter 1. And you can't hurry love or acquisition.

What if you are tied to a textbook?

Many teachers out there have little or no control over the materials they use in class, and if that's your case, it's normal to feel as if everything we have said in this book is not applicable to your situation. However, if the only thing you cannot change is the textbook, then the answer is relatively simple: Textbooks can (and should!) be supplemented by the types of activities we have showcased in this book. And beyond the specific examples we have provided, keep in mind the main principles we have outlined. Making sure students are able and compelled to understand and convey meaning is not exclusive to TBLT or IPAs, and it is not limited to specific thematic units either.

Believe it or not, using a textbook is a constraint that can be overcome. As popular as it has become to dislike textbooks, it is also true that instructors appreciate having textbooks as "guides" in terms of what to do or what to talk about. Just ditching the textbook won't make your curriculum magically better, and using a textbook does not mean you are doomed to a traditional approach. The real issue arises when you cannot change the way students are assessed or evaluated.

If you are obligated to use tests that follow a traditional approach based on rote memorization as opposed to assessing the students' communicative abilities, then the best answer we can give you is to use what you now know to push for change. Otherwise, if you only change the activities you do in class, but students continue to be assessed through discrete-point items, then your efforts will likely lead to student frustration (i.e., "our teacher is not teaching us!") and skepticism on the part of your admins or supervisors (i.e., "this communicative stuff is not helping them!").

What if my students seem disengaged?

First and foremost, survey your students to see if your perceptions are accurate. For instance, just because some learners are quiet, that doesn't mean they're disengaged. You may find that they are enjoying the class more than you think. And, by the way, surveying your students from time to time is a good idea, even if students appear to be highly engaged.

Second, if they are indeed disengaged, it is important to understand why. Many times, students feel disengaged when the activities seem too difficult or too easy. If they feel as if they are struggling, it is good to ask them more specifically what they find the most challenging, as well as what they have found helpful in the past (or in other lessons). If they don't feel challenged enough, adjust how fast you talk, expand the selection of texts, and increase autonomy by allowing them to be more in charge of their own learning.

If the issue is not so much the level, but rather, the format, topics, or content, ask them what topics they like to learn about, what types of texts they prefer (e.g., short stories, graphic novels, news articles, short films, documentaries, interviews, etc.) and what types of activities they tend to enjoy (e.g., games, creative tasks, mini-projects, etc.). Of course, as we indicated in Chapter 2, you cannot let your learners dictate the entire curriculum, and you might not be able to change everything, but there may be ways of including information that they find interesting.

External circumstances might also be a cause of disengagement. As Cook (2008) said, "In an ideal teachers' world, students would enter the classroom admiring the target culture and language, wanting to get something out of the second language learning for themselves, eager to experience the benefits of bilingualism and thirsting for knowledge" (p. 139). However, the reality for many educators is far from that ideal. If students are taking your course only to fulfill a graduation requirement, and they seem quite vocal about their lack of interest, the best advice we can give you is to listen. In a way, this situation is somewhat analogous with colleagues resistant to changing how they teach! When we don't feel heard or acknowledged, and someone continues to impose something on us, we are bound to resist even more. Explore more flexible ways for them to demonstrate their learning. For instance, contract learning (i.e., students and instructors negotiate and agree on what they want to work on and accomplish), could be a good way for them to shift their focus away from just getting a passing grade.

Disengagement can also be a symptom of unmet expectations. Students may have preconceived notions of what should take place in a language class, and instead of confronting you about why you're not doing what they think you should be doing, they mentally check out. Rather than assuming that your students will understand why you do what you do, explicitly state your learning goals and how you plan to help students achieve them. As obvious as some things might be to you, they may not be obvious to students. Sometimes, they need to see the connection between what you do in class and how they will be assessed, and, preferably, in the near future. Other times, they need to understand how completing a particular task will be helpful on a broader ("real world") level. Of course, you might need to first make sure that your Can-Do Statements are also relevant and useful for students, as opposed to "we have to do this because it's what ACTFL says we should do."

On a related note, don't forget that "just to practice" is not a compelling purpose. Ask yourself: What's the point? Limit display questions to a minimum, and instead focus on interpreting and expressing meaning for a real purpose, like finding out something you don't know.

Last, but not least, variety is the spice of life. You don't need to come up with a new idea for every lesson, but having learners do something different from time to time will liven things up. Games and competitions are always a fun way to break up the monotony while continuing to engage learners in meaningful interpretation and expression of meaning (e.g., meme contest, trivia game, logic puzzles, etc.). Trying new tech tools can also add variety, but be selective and don't overdo it. Learning how to use new platforms can be overwhelming for instructors and students alike. If you are not particularly adventurous when it comes to integrating technology, seek recommendations from colleagues, not only about which tools to try, but more importantly, what to do with them. Our mantra when it comes to technology is: Start with the task, and then choose the tool.

What if students appear to be at different proficiency levels?

Let's state the obvious: We all teach mixed-level classes! Language development is not uniform, and yet in most educational settings, we seem to be expected to teach and assess uniformly. However, more and more educators realize the importance of differentiated instruction, which essentially consists of strategies to help each student develop their language skills while being equally challenged and engaged. Easier said than done? In most cases, yes. However, here are a few suggestions we can offer.

First, focus on what everyone can benefit from. For example, providing useful vocabulary and sentence stems when completing a writing or speaking activity can help all students, as long as they are free to choose whether to use that or not. Something else we know all learners benefit from is reading: If you have a classroom library, incorporate a free voluntary reading program as part of your course.

Indeed, giving students choices whenever possible is a key aspect of differentiated instruction. For interpretive activities, you can provide at least two choices of texts (videos, songs, readings, etc.) on the same topic, even if they don't contain identical information. In fact, you could have students compare and contrast the information they learned. We understand that finding and providing multiple resources is not always feasible, though.

For presentational activities, students could have different prompts to choose from. For instance, some students feel more comfortable and motivated to work on a creative topic, whereas others might prefer an expository task, where they are summarizing or reporting information. In addition, try to give students the freedom to determine how they complete the task: a video, a live presentation, an infographic, a short paragraph, etc. That being said, it is important to strive for a balance of modalities (oral, written) across all three modes of communication.

When it comes to computer-graded activities, you can let students choose a certain number of them (e.g., "out of the 10 vocab activities, complete at least five of them"), or you can have some required activities for everyone and an additional set of questions as optional practice for students who need it. Online assignments are indeed a great way to differentiate instruction: Students not only advance at their own pace, but also receive individualized feedback.

Last, but not least, put students in charge of their own learning—and teaching! For example, you can have learners lead small "book clubs," where each group picks what they will read, and every week, a different group member leads the discussion on each chapter. Similarly, instead of traditional presentations, have students prepare games that everyone can play in class (with your guidance!).

Wrapping Up

Most SLA and language pedagogy books, including this one, make the authors seem as if they have it all figured out. Just do what we say, right? The reality is that any advice given without a nuanced consideration of the instructional context is bound to need some adaptation. It is impossible for us, or any other author, blogger, or workshop facilitator, to tell you exactly what you should be doing at all times. Our goal was not to plan every class for you, but rather to provide the foundation or reassurance needed for you to (re)examine and (re)discover your approach. Make our ideas your own, and share your success with others!

Works Cited

Adair-Hauck, B., Glisan, E., & Troyan, F. (2013). *Implementing integrated performance assessment.* ACTFL.

Adams, R. (2007). Do second language learners benefit from interacting with each other? In A. Mackey (Ed.), *Conversational interaction in second language acquisition* (pp. 29–51). Oxford University Press.

American Council on the Teaching of Foreign Languages (ACTFL). (2012a). *Proficiency guidelines.* ACTFL.

American Council on the Teaching of Foreign Languages (ACTFL). (2012b). *Performance descriptors for language learners.* ACTFL.

Birulés-Muntané, J., & Soto-Faraco, S. (2016). Watching subtitled films can help learning foreign languages. *PLoS One, 11.*

Cook, V. (2008). *Second language learning and language teaching.* Hodder Education.

Crane, C. (2016). Making connections in beginning language instruction through structured reflection and the world-readiness standards for learning languages. In P. Urlaub & J. Watzinger-Tharp (Eds.), *The interconnected language curriculum: Critical transitions and interfaces in articulated K–16 contexts* (pp. 51–74). Heinle.

Deardorff, D. K. (2006). Identification and assessment of intercultural competence as a student outcome of internationalization. *Journal of Studies in International Education, 10*(3), 241–66.

DeKeyser, R. (2014). Skill acquisition theory. In B. VanPatten & J. Williams (Eds.), *Theories in second language acquisition: An introduction* (pp. 94–112). Routledge.

Dörnyei, Z. (1994). Motivation and motivating in the foreign language classroom. *The Modern Language Journal, 78*(3), 273–84.

Ellis, R. (2008). A typology of written corrective feedback types. *ELT Journal, 63,* 97–107.

Ellis, R. (2009). Task-based language teaching: Sorting out the misunderstandings. *International Journal of Applied Linguistics, 19*(3), 221–46.

Ellis, R. & Shintani, N. (2014). *Exploring language pedagogy through second language acquisition research.* Routledge.

Ellis, R., Skehan, P., Li, S., Shintani, N., & Lambert, C. (2019). *Task-based language teaching: Theory and practice.* Cambridge University Press.

Fernández, C. (2016). Effectively addressing forces that resist positive changes to improve language learning. *The Language Educator, 11,* 50–52.

Ferris, D. (1999). The case for grammar correction in L2 writing classes: A response to Truscott (1996). *Journal of Second Language Writing, 8*(1), 1–11.

Flower, L., & Hayes, J. (1981). A cognitive process theory of writing. *College Composition and Communication, 32*(4), 365–87.

Grabe, W. (2014). Key issues in L2 reading development. *Centre for English Language Communication,* 8–18.

Graham, S. & Macaro, E. (2008). Strategy instruction in listening for lower-intermediate learners of French. *Language Learning, 58*(4), 747–83.

Grosjean F. (1989). Neurolinguists, beware! The bilingual is not two monolinguals in one person. *Brain and Language, 36*(1), 3–15.

Hayati, A. & Mohmedi, F. (2011). The effect of films with and without subtitles on listening comprehension of EFL learners. *British Journal of Educational Technology, 42*, 181–92.

Henshaw, F. (2020). Online translators in language classes: Pedagogical and practical considerations. *FLTMAG*.

Horst, M., Cobb, T., & Meara, P. (1998). Beyond a clockwork orange: Acquiring second language vocabulary through reading. *Reading in a Foreign Language, 11*, 207–23.

Jeon, E.H. & Yamashita, J. (2014). L2 reading comprehension and its correlates: A meta-analysis. *Language Learning, 64*(1), 160–212.

Keating, G. (2016). *Second language acquisition: The basics*. Routledge.

Kern, R. (1989), Second language reading strategy instruction: Its effects on comprehension and word inference ability. *The Modern Language Journal, 73*(2), 135–49.

Krashen, S. (1985). *The input hypothesis: Issues and implications*. Longman.

Krashen, S. (1996), The case for narrow listening, *System, 24*(1), 97–100.

Lee, J. & VanPatten, B. (2003). *Making communicative language teaching happen*. McGraw-Hill.

Lightbown, P. (2003). SLA research in the classroom/SLA research for the classroom. *Language Learning Journal, 28*(1), 4–13.

Long, M. (1985). A role for instruction in second language acquisition: Task-based language teaching. In K. Hylstenstam & M. Pienemann (Eds.), *Modelling and assessing second language acquisition* (pp. 77–99). Multilingual Matters.

Long, M. (1991). Focus on form: A design feature in language teaching methodology. In K. De Bot, R. Ginsberg, & C. Kramsch (Eds.), *Foreign language research in cross-cultural perspectives* (pp. 39–52). John Benjamins.

Long, M. (1996). The role of the linguistic environment in second language acquisition. In W. C. Ritchie & T. K. Bhatia (Eds.), *Handbook of second language acquisition* (pp. 413–68). Academic Press.

National Standards Collaborative Board (2015). *World-readiness standards for learning languages*. ACTFL.

Philp, J. (2003). Constraints on "noticing the gap": Nonnative speakers' noticing of recasts in NS-NNS interaction. *Studies in Second Language Acquisition, 25*(1), 99–126.

Polio, C. The relevance of second language acquisition theory to the written error correction debate, *Journal of Second Language Writing, 21*(4), 375–89.

Randi, J. Grigorenko, E. & Sternberg, R. (2005). *Revisiting definitions of reading comprehension: Just what is reading comprehension anyway?* Routledge.

Sato, M. & Loewen, S. (2019). *Evidence-based second language pedagogy: A collection of instructed second language acquisition studies*. Routledge.

Sato, M., & Lyster, R. (2007). Modified output of Japanese EFL learners: Variable effects of interlocutor vs. feedback types. In A. Mackey (Ed.), *Conversational interaction in second language acquisition: A series of empirical studies* (pp. 123–42). Oxford University Press.

Spada, N. (1997). Form-focused instruction and second language acquisition: A review of classroom and laboratory research. *Language Teaching, 30*(2), 73–87.

Spada, N. and Lightbown, P. (2008). Form-focused instruction: Isolated or integrated? *TESOL Quarterly, 42*(8), 181–207.

Sparks, R. (2019). Why reading is a challenge for US L2 learners: The impact of cognitive, ecological, and psychological factors in L2 comprehension. *Foreign Language Annals, 52*(4), 727–43.

Storch, N. & Aldosari, A. (2013). Pairing learners in pair work activity. *Language Teaching Research, 17*(1), 31–48.

Storch, N. & Aldosari, K. (2019). Peer feedback: An activity theory perspective on givers' and receivers' stances. In M. Sato & S. Loewen (Eds.), *Evidence-based second language pedagogy* (pp. 123–44). Routledge.

Swaffar, J., Arens, K. & Byrnes, H. (1991). *Reading for meaning: An integrated approach to language learning.* Prentice-Hall.

Swain, M. (1985). Communicative competence: Some roles of comprehensible input and comprehensible output in its development. In S. Gass & C. Madden (Eds.), *Input in second language acquisition* (pp. 235–56). Newbury House.

Swain, M. (2000). The output hypothesis and beyond: Mediating acquisition through collaborative dialogue. In J. P. Lantolf (Ed.), *Sociocultural theory and second language learning* (pp. 97–114). Oxford University Press.

Taylor, G. (2005). Perceived processing strategies of students watching captioned video. *Foreign Language Annals, 38*(3), 422–27.

Truscott, J. (1996). The case against grammar correction in L2 writing classes. *Language Learning, 46*(2), 327–69.

Vandergrift, L. (2004). Learning to listen or listening to learn. *Annual Review of Applied Linguistics, 24*, 3–25.

Vandergrift, L. & Tafaghodtari, M. H. (2010). Teaching learners how to listen does make a difference: An empirical study. *Language Learning 65*, 470–97.

VanPatten, B. (1996). *Input processing and grammar instruction: Theory and research.* Ablex.

VanPatten, B. (2003). *From input to output: A teacher's guide to second language acquisition.* McGraw-Hill.

VanPatten, B. (2017). *While we're on the topic: BVP on language, acquisition, and classroom practice.* ACTFL.

Webb, S. (2007). The effects of repetition on vocabulary knowledge. *Applied Linguistics, 28*, 46–65.

Weir, C. J. (1990). *Communicative language testing.* Prentice Hall.

Wiggins, G., & McTighe, J. (2005). *Understanding by design.* Association for Supervision and Curriculum Development.

Wong, W. & VanPatten, B. (2003). The evidence is IN: Drills are OUT. *Foreign Language Annals, 36*(3), 403–23.

Zhao, S. Y., & Bitchener, J. (2007). Incidental focus on form in teacher-learner and learner-learner interactions. *System, 35*(4), 431–47.